Paul Wheatley

Munich: From Monks to Modernity

Right: map of Munich from 1806 by Johann Carl Schleich, created in conjunction with an 1801-initiated project to accurately map the whole of Bavaria

Paul Wheatley

Munich: From Monks to Modernity

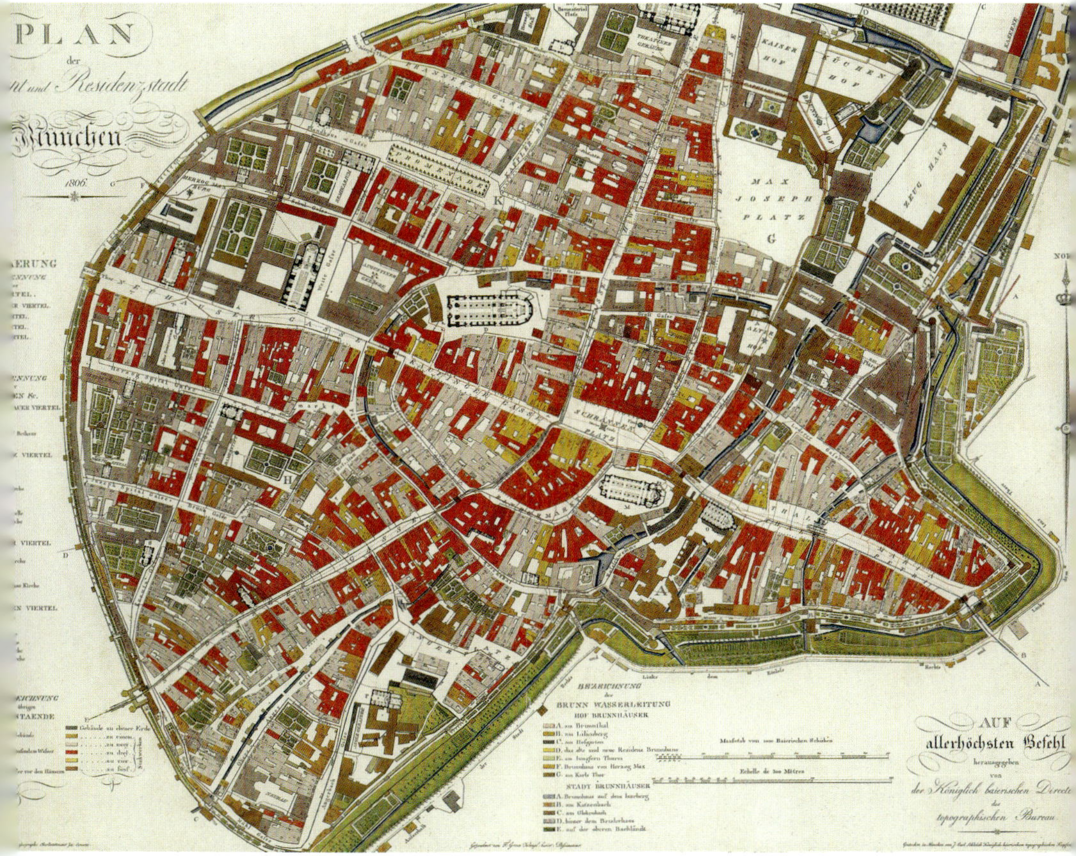

Volk Verlag München

Streitfeldstraße 19, 81673 München
Tel.: 089/420 79 69 80, Fax: 089/420 79 69 80
www.volkverlag.de

Druck: Auer GmbH Donauwörth
Printed in Germany

Die Deutsche Bibliothek verzeichnet diese Publikation in der Deutschen Nationalbibliografie; detaillierte bibliografische Daten sind im Internet über http://dnb.ddb.de abrufbar

ISBN 978-3-937200-88-0

Contents

PART 2: THE PATH TO MODERNITY

Introduction

'Here we are in Munich,' wrote the excited British art student Anna Mary Howitt on 1 June 1850, the day of her arrival in the city. 'These last several days,' she explained, 'have been such a confusion of excitement, disappointment, joy, fatigue and disgust, that I barely know where to begin my narrative.'

From a 21st-century perspective, mid-19th-century Munich can appear to have been characterised by an almost naive charm. It was capital of a Bavaria that was by then a kingdom, raised from an electorate, albeit by the grace of Napoleon Bonaparte in 1806, though by the time Howitt arrived in the city it was still largely recognisable as the medieval settlement that until recently it had been. This was a post-Ludwig I period, whose patronage of artists and architects had helped lift the status of Munich to that of a genuine *Kunststadt*, a city of art. By the 1880s, Munich was widely recognised as Germany's most important art location, symbolised – mythologised, perhaps – by the 'Bohemian Schwabing' quarter. Though *fin de siècle* Munich was struggling to stay ahead of its great rival, Berlin, as the pre-eminent art city of the German Empire, it was, nevertheless, home to writers of the calibre of Thomas Mann, art movements such as *Jugendstil* and leading abstract artists such as Wassily Kandinsky.

As with many German cities, from the 1840s Munich experienced rapid economic expansion and huge population growth, though industrialisation was on a much more modest scale than that found, for example, in Berlin and the Ruhr areas of Germany. Throughout this period of great flux, Mun ich managed to maintain the appearance of holding onto its beauty while modernising in its own unique way. Beer became a mainstay of the economy, as did locomotive building, while the city became a regional financial centre. On the whole, however, the image wonderfully painted in Anna Mary Howitt's *An Art Student in Munich* was still eminently recognisable even in the pre-First World War city.

Then the caesura of 1914-1918 radically changes the historical narrative.

Since the city's foundation in the latter half of the 1150s, the prevailing image had been of a city shaped by Catholicism, a city of art, with great baroque and rococo architecture, not forgetting the all too pervasive strivings of various Bavarian rulers for wider European influence. In reality, Munich had never been much more than the capital of a state that was little more than a regional power, hemmed in by the superpowers of Austria and France, and later Prussia, which it surrendered to in the form of the German Empire in 1871, and which lasted until the catastrophe of 1914-1918.

There were, of course, many continuities between pre-First World War Munich and the city during the Weimar Republic. But the combined impact of Germany's defeat in the First World War and the subsequent Bavarian revolution radicalised many in the city, and Munich became an attractive haven for right-wing extremists. It is at this point that the failures of German democracy in the form of the Weimar Republic leap out of history books, pointing at Munich, Adolf Hitler and the creation of the Third Reich.

The city was central to the rise of the Nazis, the subsequent catastrophe of the Second World War and the Holocaust. Indeed, the Third Reich continues to be central to the city's self-understanding. Problems arise, however, when the Third Reich comes to determine a city's history to such an extent that it leaves little room for anything else. Just as there is with any other city, there is more than one side to the history of Munich.

I came to Munich from a background studying European history, focusing on Germany, and I gravitated as a postgraduate into studying Bavaria. The onset of Munich's 850th birthday celebrations in 2008 fascinated me, encompassing as they did periods, epochs and personalities I only vaguely recognised: Heinrich der Löwe, the city's founder in the 12th century; Ludwig der Bayer, the city's first Holy Roman Emperor; the American born British reformer-scientist, Sir Benjamin Thompson; Count Maximilian Joseph von Montgelas, who pushed Bavaria towards much-needed modernisation; Ludwig I, the city's greatest art patron, brought down by Lola Montez, an Irish dancer; great scientists, such as Carl von Linde, whose work on refrigeration facilitated the rise of the Munich brewery industry, and Max von Pettenkofer, who transformed public health in the city; the revolutionary though eminently tragic Kurt Eisner; all the way to popular post-war Munich mayor Thomas Wimmer and current long-serving mayor, Christian Ude.

But with the exception of the ubiquitous Nazis, what else do most non-Germans know about the city? Most know Bayern Munich football club, business people may have visited the city due to it being Germany's pre-eminent high-tech business location. Many others know the city as home to the Oktoberfest, or at least the inside of a beer tent at the Oktoberfest, and the usual stereotypical image of lederhosen and dirndl.

This book is aimed at general readers wanting to know more about a city that has much more to offer than *Gemütlichkeit*, Weißwurst and National Socialism. This is a gentle dash through the city's history and it encompasses a wide range of subjects. In as much as is possible in just over 200 pages, it pertains to be a synthesis and therefore relies on books, articles, newspaper reports and witness accounts of the history of the city. The first half of the book is something more of a narrative and it does not attempt to come up with new theories about particular 'turning points', and it does not delve too deeply into underlying causes. This first half contains four chapters encompassing epochs from the city's foundation to the present day: 1158-1648 (foundation to the end of the Thirty Years War); 1648-1815 (up to the end of the Napoleonic era); 1815-1945 (up to the end of the Second World War); 1945-2010 (to the present day). The second half of the book follows three thematic routes through the history of the city: industry and economy; art, architecture and place; beer and football.

The narrative is supplemented by a series of interviews I conducted between summer 2008 and late 2009 with a wide range of people considered Munich 'experts' in some way. At times the interviews find their way into the running narrative, other times as additional stand-alone boxes, the aim being to provide a contemporary and supplementary snapshot opinion on the city. I would like to thank, then, the following for taking the time to answer my questions, setting up the interviews or providing help during a particularly hectic two years from the conception of this project to printing. As well as to Michael Volk from Volk Verlag, and Florian Wagner for the cover concept, many thanks to the Bayerische Fußball-Verband, Elke Doppelbauer, Sebastian Eichle, Regina Geibel, Professor Wolfgang Heckl, Raphael Honigstein, Professor Sir Ian Kershaw, Dr Dieter Klein, Philipp Lahm, Marian Offman, Ellen Presser, Juliane Riedl, Dr Freimut Scholz, Renate Schostack, Dr Michael Stephan, the Verein Münchener Brauereien and Bernhard Weidemann. Any errors are my responsibility alone but I fully appreciate the efforts of Dankó Szabo for finding the time in a busy schedule to run his expert eye over the manuscript. I would also like to offer an extra thank you to historian Dr Graham Ford for offering advice and suggestions at a late stage in the writing process. It is through the efforts of Dr Ford and his colleagues on a not-so-young undergraduate that my fumbling interest in history was transformed into a passion.

Paul Wheatley
Munich, November 2009

PART 1
HISTORY

The 'Augsburger Schied': Friedrich Barbarossa's 'Augsburg Decision' of 14 June 1158 confirmed the establishment of Munich

Chapter 1

FOUNDATION TO THE THIRTY YEARS WAR (1158-1648)

~

A Violent Beginning?

The attackers probably struck under cover of darkness, early morning or late at night, perhaps concealed until the last moment by a covering of dense fog. Sent by Duke Heinrich XII der Löwe ('the Lion') of Bavaria (1129-1195), some were on horseback, most probably all were armed with weapons ranging from swords and bows to daggers and fiery torches. The aim? Simple: destroy and burn the flourishing market town and toll bridge at Föhring, which Bishop Otto I of Freising (c.1111-1158) had established there in 1140. In short, the small Föhring population stood little chance against Heinrich's men.

This attack took place some time between 1156 and 1158, and it signifies the dramatic early steps in what was to become the city of Munich. Today, Föhring is a Munich suburb, under the name of Oberföhring, another town gobbled up by an ever-expanding city in the late 19th and early 20th centuries. Over 850 years ago, Föhring seemed – to the Bishop of Freising, at least – to be the ideal location for the all-important transportation of salt over the river Isar on its way from Reichenhall and Salzburg (both around 110 kilometres south-east of Munich as the crow flies) to Augsburg (around 35 kilometres north-east of Munich). To Heinrich der Löwe, however, who had been granted Bavaria in 1156 by Holy Roman Emperor Friedrich I (1122-1190), better known as 'Barbarossa', it presented a significant hindrance to his wresting total control of the lucrative mint, market and toll on the banks of the Isar.

Freising, similar to Munich, is today part of the southern German state of Bavaria. Back then, in the 1150s, the area was part of a prince-bishopric, ruled and controlled by the Bishop of Freising, the power-hungry uncle of Friedrich Barbarossa. Bishop Otto, a prince from the House of Babenberg, was one of the most important European writers, historians and thinkers of the 12th century, though he rarely confined himself to matters of the Catholic Church. In

Contemporary Munich: with the most recognisable image of the Medieval Altstadt, the 99-metre-high Frauenkirche

addition to his expertise in spiritual and religious matters, Otto was a first-rate political and strategic thinker, which he exercised in order to extend his influence and gain privileges for his bishopric. It was this striving for influence and power that propelled him to construct the toll bridge at Föhring and claim the considerable income from the passage of 'white gold': salt. Everything was going to plan, it seems, until the arrival of Heinrich and his henchmen, who, after destroying Föhring, transferred the salt crossing eight kilometres upstream (south) to the tiny existing settlement of 'die villa Munichen', Munich.

If Otto's lust for power and influence was considerable, it was firmly put in the shade by that of Heinrich der Löwe. Similar to Otto, Heinrich was closely related to Emperor Barbarossa, in this case as a cousin. Black-haired with dark eyes, Heinrich came from the Welf dynasty, and by the 1150s he had become, after Barbarossa, the most powerful person in the Holy Roman Empire, characterised by his Freising adversary as ruling from 'sea to sea, from Denmark to Sicily'. For Heinrich, however, Bavaria was little more than a southern adjunct to his real centre of power, in Braunschweig, today Lower Saxony, northern Germany. Indeed, how important Bavaria was to Heinrich can be gauged from the fact that he only ever visited seven times.

To celebrate the 850th anniversary of Heinrich's founding of Munich, in 2008 the city held numerous grand festivals and celebrations, and a number of books were published on the city's history. But what of Munich's violent foundation story? The first-known document mentioning Munich is the so-called Augsburger Schied, or 'Augsburg Decision', of 14 June 1158, nowadays referred to as Munich's 'foundation document'. This is the document that Emperor Barbarossa is believed to have issued in order to rubber-stamp Heinrich's transfer of the bridge from Föhring to Munich and the establishment of a mint and market there. Significantly, though, the document does not mention the destruction of the bridge at Föhring. As well as retroactively approving of Heinrich's action, the Augsburg document also instructed the duke to pay one third of his income from Munich to the Bishop of Freising, a payment that in one form or another continued until 1802.

Heinrich's good favour with Barbarossa, however, did not last, and he lost not just Bavaria but much of his land in Saxony on the orders of the emperor. A second Barbarossa document of 1180, again from Augsburg, confirmed Heinrich's loss of Bavaria and ordered the transfer of the bridge, mint and market back to Föhring. Most historians agree the reason that this was never carried out was due to the fact that Munich was by then a flourishing economic settlement.

While the celebration date for Munich's foundation refers to the date of the Augsburg Decision of 14 June 1158, the actual date of the transfer of the bridge was probably some time in 1156 or 1157, though there is little concrete evidence to say for certain. A further uncertainty from this period is the nature of the settlements in the area before Munich's foundation. Surrounding areas were certainly inhabited: prior to 1158, a crossing over the river Isar linked settlements at nearby Haidhausen, Laim and Pasing, and crossed the area where Munich's inner city would later emerge. Moreover, it is probable that Munich is a derivation from the German word *Mönche*, meaning 'monks', who were living in this area of the river Isar. Which monks were there and from when is harder to ascertain. Documentary evidence indicates that various cloisters were established in the locality from the 8th century, most nota-

Dr Michael Stephan, former Director of the Bavarian State Archive, now Senior Director of the Munich City Archive

On the Bavarian State Archive and the Munich City Archive
The Bavarian administration produces documentation, and after 10, 20, 30 years it needs to be archived. The archives are a mirror of the administration of the state of Bavaria. In December [2008] I move to the [Munich] City Archive, and the files are a mirror of the administration of Munich. The Bavarian archive has the documents from the state chancellor's office, the Staatskanzlei, and the ministries. We collect the private papers from the ministers and ministries and other people important to Bavarian history.

On Freimut Scholz's (see page 17) theory of the foundation of Munich
I know him very well. I made an exhibition in August [2008] about the same theme … I have had many discussions with Freimut Scholz. My opinion is that the old explanation is right … I have a political explanation for the events of 1158. It was a political show … It is more logical because of the contradiction [between the two Augsburg documents]. In the first document there is no word about the bridge. Twenty-two years later [there was]. Why then? The explanation is that it was a political decision from the emperor not to mention the case in the first document because he wanted peace. It is a 'peaceful' document because it is a treaty. Both partners [Heinrich and the Bishop of Freising] had a share from the incomes from the bridge and the tolls. But the political situation changed in 1180. Heinrich der Löwe was deposed and the Emperor didn't have to consider him any more. That's why there is the contradiction between the two documents.

On the importance of salt to the city's history
Salt was the most important trade and the wealth of Munich was based on it: the wealth of Munich merchants and also the wealth of Bavarian dukes. Later, the dukes fully realised the importance of salt and thought that it could be even more important for themselves, and salt became a state monopoly, both the production and trading … If you go to the Hofgarten [Royal Court Gardens], there is a little temple, and a statue of Bavaria. In one of her arms is a deer and at her feet is a barrel of salt, which signifies that the wealth of Bavaria was from salt from the Alps.

On the pitfalls of writing about Munich
Not to prolong the stereotypes about Munich. If it's Munich: Weißwürst, beer, lederhosen … Munich is a small but global-thinking capital and it's too easy to reduce it to these. Though it's very difficult to fight against these stereotypes because it's like a corporate identity.

bly the Benedictine Cloister Schaftlärn, founded in 762. It is also posited that in 782 settlements at nearby Sendling and Schwabing, today areas of Munich, were given to Cloister Schäftlarn by a member of the local nobility.

There is, however, an interesting aside to the prevailing narrative about Heinrich der Löwe and Munich's violent beginning. Dr Freimut Scholz has worked for several years on official exhibitions (predominately for the Stadtmuseum) about the history of the city. Over this period he has become convinced that the evidence for the foundation of Munich has been badly misinterpreted, and with it so ingrained in the psyche of the city that it is almost unchallengeable.

His thesis has been published in the history journal *Zeitschrift für Bayerische Landesgeschichte* and also in a 2008 book. According to Scholz's hypothosis, the 'violent' beginning to Munich's history that is taught to Munich's school children and repeated in so many publications is inaccurate. The pivotal point, according to Scholz, is that when Emperor Friedrich Barbarossa's 1158 Augsburg Decision was enacted, the bridge at Föhring had not yet been destroyed. Therefore, rather than the outcome of an act of violence by Heinrich der Löwe, Munich's foundation was agreed by Barbarossa, Heinrich and Bishop Otto of Freising prior to the transfer of the bridge from Föhring to Munich. It is too early to tell whether this hypothosis will prevail, but Scholz's perhaps seemingly 'old-fashioned' but valuable document-based research should be welcomed for engendering worthy debate on the city's foundation story.

A Flourishing City

Whilst on 11 November 1918, after four years of carnage in the First World War, the major powers of Britain, the US and France were celebrating victory against Germany and the Austro-Hungarian Empire, Germany was already engulfed by revolutionary fervour. Among the royal houses that were toppled in those weeks was the Bavarian House of Wittelsbach, a dynasty that had survived wars, invasions, pestilence, penury, incompetence and just about everything else history could fling at it since being handed power in the 12th century.

On the fall of Heinrich der Löwe in 1180, Emperor Barbarossa named Otto I von Wittelsbach (1120-1183) as duke of Bavaria, though similar to Heinrich before him he also had to share the profits from the mint and customs with the Bishop of Freising. This first ever Wittelsbach ruler of Bavaria, along with his son Ludwig I (1174-1231), oversaw the first stages of an upswing in the incipient market centre of Munich, and documentary evidence suggests that Munich had already received city status by the early decades of the 13th century. Ludwig I's successor, Otto II, built on these foundations and by 1240 had succeeded in chipping away at the Bishop of Freising's influence in Munich to such an extent that the Wittelsbachs soon became the undisputed rulers of the city.

As well as the legacy of a name, in 1239 monks were also the inspiration behind Munich's coat of arms, which featured a monk's head wearing a typical cowl, below an eagle atop city gates. A monk invariably appeared on the city's coat of arms thereafter, though sometime around the 16th century it was transformed into – but not superseded by – a child-like figure, which eventually became known as the 'Münchner Kindl', or 'Munich child'. The coat of arms has had a number of official and unofficial manifestations and designs, usually featuring a monk figure with arms outstretched, a red book in its left hand (sometimes replaced with a beer glass or radish). It was not until 1957, in fact, that the city council stipulated that the official coat of arms should be derived from a 1313 version, which means it should now display a monk-like figure in black cowl with gold decoration, red book in outstretched left hand and red feet. Whether it is the Münchner Kindl or the official monk, the ubiquitous coat of arms can be seen across the city today adorning anything from manhole covers and lampposts to advertisements and beer glasses.

Even earlier than the coat of arms, a version of Munich's first church, St Peter's, was already in existence in the 12th century. This was replaced in 1284 by a new St Peter's, which, after burning to the ground in the great fire of 1327, was replaced by a third and final St Peter's, consecrated in 1368. A new church, Unserer Lieben Frau, erected shortly before 1250 (on the same location as today's Frauenkirche), signifies that Munich was becoming an increasingly affluent city with a growing population. At this time, the settlement was separated between the diocese of St Peter's and that of Unserer Lieben Frau by today's Neuhauser Straße, Kaufingerstraße and Tal (from Stachus to Isartor). Moreover, pointing to the position the city would hold as a Catholic redoubt, by the 1290s Munich already had three cloisters: Franciscan (rebuilt 1284),

Monks adorn numerous buildings and objects around the city. The left hangs from a bridge and the right is a stained-glass window in the Neues Rathaus

Augustiner (1290) and St Jakob Anger Cloister, which possibly pre-dated Munich's foundation.

In 1255 Bavaria was partitioned between two branches of the Wittelsbach family: Ludwig II der Strenge (1229-1294; der Strenge, 'the severe' because he had his first wife, Marie of Brabant, killed in the mistaken belief she had comitted adultery) ruling in Upper Bavaria (Oberbayern) and the Palatine on the river Rhine (Pfalzgrafschaft bei Rhein), with Munich as its capital; and Heinrich XIII (1235-1290) ruling Lower Bavaria (Niederbayern), with its capital in Landshut.

With Munich confirmed as the capital of Upper Bavaria, Duke Ludwig II set about enlarging his residence, today's Alter Hof (which dates back to the late 12th century), extending the size of the city as well as starting a huge new wall circumventing the settlement. By the end of the 13th century, the city's population totalled around 10,000, meaning it had swiftly become the most populous city in Upper Bavaria and with it relatively wealthy, evidenced by the city's tax doubling that of the second-placed city, Ingolstadt. There were even years in which Munich's tax receipts exceeded those of all other Upper Bavarian cities and towns put together, which, of course, meant the duke received huge sums of money on the back of the city's increasing wealth. The city received a further economic boost when in 1280 it was handed significant trading privileges, similar to those enjoyed by more well-established cities in the Holy Roman Empire, including the nearby, far wealthier and much more important free Imperial city (*Reichsstadt*) of Regensburg.

On Ludwig II's death in 1294 his successor was to be his 12-year-old son, also called Ludwig (1281-1347), but on account of his age, his third wife's son, 19-year-old Rudolf (1274-1319), took on the official role of the young heir's guardian and eventually later that year became Duke Rudolf I of Bavaria. Rudolf lent his name to the 22 articles of the *Rudolfinum*, which is seen as comprising Munich's 'foundation laws' or first 'constitution' (often compared to England's Magna Carta). By 1286, Munich already had some sort of *Rat*, or council, albeit with severely restricted powers, and the *Rudolfinum* entrusted the government of Munich to a 12-man Inner Council, drawn from Munich's approximately 20 leading patrician families, for example: Impler, Kaufinger and Sendlinger, today familiar as street names. At various times, representatives of the families occupied seats on the all-important Munich Inner Council as well as holding the position of mayor. Some of these, the richest families in the city, dealt in the salt or fabric trades, others in gold. In contrast, artisans and craftsmen (who, from the 14th century, were organised into guilds and important to the city's wealth) had little real political influence.

Munich's development as a south German economic axis was built on the crucial legal right that from 1332 salt had to be stored in the city prior to its transportation farther north. In effect, an extremely lucrative salt monopoly. Wealth from the salt trade attracted other businesses throughout the 14th and 15th centuries, particularly in expensive fabrics, such as silk, velvet and brocade. Much of this trade was carried out at Munich's most important market, today's Marienplatz, then known simply as Marktplatz. In addition to lucrative gold and fabric transactions, this bustling marketplace was also a hive of buying and selling, with stalls offering anything from vegetables, bread and meat to wine, shoes and clothes.

While Munich's population was susceptible to an early and arbitrary death through disease, particularly to the plague, which hit the city 25 times between 1349 and 1860, harvest failures hit the poor hardest. Fire was an additional hazard. With the exception of some churches and a small handful of other buildings, the city consisted of little but wooden constructions. To varying degrees, then, fire left parts of the city in ashes in 1221, 1327 (which destroyed up to a third of the city, including the Franciscan cloister) and, in a terrible first half of the 15th century, also in 1407, 1418 (consuming the Tal area), 1429 (destroying a huge area between today's Promenadeplatz and Neuhauser Straße) and 1434. The 1327 fire prompted Ludwig IV to issue Munich's first significant building regulations, decreeing wider streets and the greater use of brick rather than wood in future constructions.

As well as the trading rights of 1280, a strong Jewish presence in the city was in some respects indicative of a flourishing trading centre, with Jewish settlements located behind the central Marktplatz in Judengasse ('Jew Alley'). Persecution of Europe's Jews in the Middle Ages was far from uncommon. In 1190, for example, in the northern English city of York (at the time England's second city, after London), a fire was blamed on the city's Jewish community, after which, angry mobs subsequently killed a number of Jews. The position of Jews in Munich proved to be every bit as precarious when in 1285 a pogrom was sparked by accusations of ritual murder. The city's Jews gathered together seeking safety in numbers at the local synagogue. Proving to be entirely inadequate for the task, it was burned to the ground, killing an estimated 60 to 150 Jews.

Similar to most towns and cities throughout Europe, Munich's Jews were occasionally welcomed, periodically persecuted, but more often than not simply banned from the city. And when the Black Death hit and devastated many parts of Europe in the middle of the 14th century, the easy scapegoat for this terrifying disease was, of course, the Jews. In 1442 they were simply banished 'for ever' from Munich.

Centre of the Holy Roman Empire

Most Britons, particularly in Scotland, recognise 1314 as an historic year: the Battle of Bannockburn, when Scotland's Robert the Bruce defeated the English and, at least for a time, ensured Scotland's independent status. Around 1,300 kilometres away, 1314 might not quite have been Munich's Bannockburn but it was certainly a monumental year for the young city. It was the year that Ludwig IV of Bavaria was elected as German king, the first Wittelsbach ever to be granted this honour.

Though the territory had been split between Upper and Lower Bavaria in 1255, Munich's position as the principal seat of the Wittelsbach dynasty solidified as the 13th century slipped into the 14th. Between 1294 and 1317, Rudolf I and Ludwig IV ruled Upper Bavaria (plus the Palatine on the Rhine) together, less than harmoniously. As noted above, Duke Rudolf I of Bavaria was the first to come of age, but he soon alienated the Munich population in a scam to add lead to coins, thus, reducing their value. Not surprisingly, the population soon realised that all that appeared to be silver was not and a furious band of malcontents responded by rioting, attacking the mint, smashing down the door and destroying the interior, prompting Rudolf to levy a huge fine on the city. Out of the siblings, however, it is not Rudolf who left the bigger mark on the city's history; Ludwig went on to oversee the 'second foundation of Munich' and is heralded as one of the most important rulers in the history of the Wittelsbach dynasty.

Though Duke Ludwig IV of Bavaria was crowned German king in 1314, and in 1328 elected Emperor of the Holy Roman Empire of the German Nation, in the 14th century there was no entity that could be identified as 'Germany', certainly not in the modern sense of a unified country with a common language and state apparatus. The Holy Roman Empire was the glue that attempted to hold together numerous small and medium-sized German and non-German lands, as well as a host of prince-bishoprics and imperial free cities. Bavaria was just one of hundreds of such lands. In 1400, the Holy Roman Empire stretched from the southern border of Denmark deep into modern Italy, including Milan and Florence. In the west, it encompassed today's Provence, Basel and the Netherlands and Belgium; in the east Vienna, Prague and swathes of modern-day Poland.

In a period in which the Holy Roman Empire has been characterised as 'enfeebled', Ludwig's reign was further complicated by the refusal of the Pope to recognise his election and his subsequent excommunication from the Catholic Church as an heretic. Moreover, it was Pope John XXII (1244-1334), based in Avignon, France, who gave Ludwig the pejorative-minded sobriquet of Ludwig der Bayer, 'the Bavarian'.

Emperors were elected by an electoral college, which in 1338 rejected papal claims to have the authority to interfere in the election process. And after the 'Golden Bull' (retrospectively named as such in the 15th century) of 1356, voting was to take place in Frankfurt-am-Main and the electors would be: the archbishops of Cologne, Mainz and Trier, plus the electors of Bohemia, Rhine

Sendlinger Tor formed part of the huge wall circumventing the Altstadt in the Middle Ages

Palatinate (a Wittelsbach), Saxony and Brandenburg, notably at this point not the duke of Bavaria.

To complicate matters for Ludwig, the day before his election as German king, on 20 October 1314, Habsburg Friedrich der Schöne ('the Handsome', 1289-1330) had been elected German king by a rival faction. Ludwig simplified matters by defeating his adversary at the Battle of Mühldorf in September 1322, Germany's last great battle comprising knights. After Friedrich recognised Ludwig's sole claim, Ludwig magnanimously invited him to share power (in a subordinate role, of course), which he rejected in favour of a return to rule purely as Austrian king. Ludwig's crowning glory – literally – should have been his coronation by a Sciarra (Giacomo) Colonna, (1270-1328) as Holy Roman Emperor in 1328 in Rome's St Peter's church. This grand setting, however, was insufficient for Ludwig, and in the hope of endowing his position as head of the Empire with greater credibility, on Whitsun of the same year, his own pope (or 'antipope'), Nicholas V (d. 1333), crowned him a second time as emperor.

With Ludwig as emperor, based in his royal residence in Munich's Alter Hof, the city became something of a focal point for a far from unified and far from coherently functioning empire. Ludwig's royal court in Munich became the centre for groups of talented theologians, philosophers and artists. Among the great names of the day, in 1328 William of Ockham (c.1285-1347), the English Franciscan monk, arrived in the city, followed by Michael of Cesena (c.1300-1342) and other Franciscans taking refuge from the Pope whilst also providing a degree of intellectual underpinning to Ludwig's disputes with the Catholic Church. In addition, more in keeping with a ducal capital, a limited but more recognisable state administration was set up, as was a ducal court, a court chapel and chancellery.

Munich gained greater municipal powers and responsibilities around this time and Ludwig bestowed trading privileges on the city, most significantly the salt monopoly in 1322. Ludwig continued the extension of the city wall and had the city's main 'gates' constructed: Schwabinger Tor, Isartor, Neuhauser Tor and Sendlinger Tor, names familiar today. The total area surrounded by the wall was around 90 hectares, though the oldest part of the city was still surrounded by an inner wall, within which the wealthy patricians lived and which was also the location of the city council. In contrast, craftsmen and traders were generally dispersed away from the centre, as were farm workers, journeymen, the poor and the infirm.

As a result of the split between upper and lower regions in 1255, even as Holy Roman Emperor, Ludwig did not rule all Bavaria. The situation changed, however, in 1340 with the death of the last Wittelsbach in Lower Bavaria, which handed Ludwig rump Bavaria (that is to say, minus the Palatinate and Upper Palatinate, which belonged to another Wittelsbach line and did not join rump Bavaria until 1777), with Munich as its capital. This unity did not last, though, and a third division in 1392 divided rump Bavaria into Bayern-Munich, Bayern-Ingolstadt and Bayern-Landshut. The impact of Munich's elevation to home of the emperor is reflected today in Munich's city colours of black and yellow (to be seen around the city, particularly during celebrations), which originate from the Empire's own coat of arms of a black eagle on a gold background. In 1347, aged 65, Emperor Ludwig died while out hunting bear, thus, bringing to an end Munich's era as the disputed centre of the Holy Roman Empire. Ludwig's reign had, however, ensured that the House of Wittelsbach was now firmly established as one of central Europe's rising dynasties.

Creating a Capital

By 1396, Munich's population was 11,267, fell to 9,488 by 1440 before climbing again to reach 12,614 in 1462 and 13,614 in 1500. This fairly modest increase by the 16th century was paralleled by a period when the city acquired an equally modest set of basic laws, which handed the city's Inner Council and Outer Council further competencies in how the city was run. Trade was expanding, and in addition to salt and fabrics, coal, stone and corn were regular staples at Munich's Marktplatz. After weathering economic difficulties in around 1400, from around the middle of the 15th century the city coffers started to record a surplus, though this was primarily the result of the lucrative salt monopoly. As well as the central market, other important city locations at this time included the centre of the salt trade at today's Promenadeplatz, from 1431 the city arsenal (today's Stadtmuseum), a brothel was established in the 1430s at am Anger, a slaughterhouse in 1465 followed soon after by a municipal bakery. In addition, in 1480 the Tanzhause (dance house) was constructed, which later served as the Rathaus, or city hall, today known as the Altes Rathaus (Old City Hall). Ulrich Fuetrer (d. 1496) decorated the building's façade, as he did the 99 coats of arms from around the world that adorn its 31-by-17-metre vault. The Altes Rathaus was also home to master sculptor Erasmus Grasser's (1450-1518) much-loved 16 Morris Dancers from 1480, which now reside in Munich's Stadtmuseum.

The 15th century additionally saw the construction of what is still Munich's most recognisable building, one that has dominated the inner city skyline ever since: Munich's Frauenkirche. Jörg von Halspach's (d.1488) monumental red-brick church, finished in 1488 (though the famous cupolas – or 'onion domes' – were not added until around 1525), was the last large-scale late-Gothic building in Bavaria and the largest 'halled-church' in southern Germany. As well as the Frauenkirche, Halspach created the Tanzhaus, renovated the Alter Hof and was also responsible for the Neuveste, which was later re-developed

Thought to be the oldest existing image of Munich, Hartmann Schedel's wonderful 1493 woodcut of the city depicts the powerful river Isar and many familiar features of the skyline (note the Frauenkirche without its cupolas)

and consumed by the Wittelsbachs' Residenz (Residence) complex. A further work of Halspach's was Schloss Blutenburg. Situated a little outside the old city in Menzing, the castle was constructed as a hunting palace and refuge for Duke Sigmund (1439-1501). Its imposing turrets and defensive-looking outer façade give it a robust appearance, though its most impressive features are the masterful interior murals by Jan Pollack (1435-1519), representing a fitting tribute to a flourishing city in the late Middle Ages.

In 1493, one year after Christopher Columbus reached the American continent, Hartmann Schedel (1440-1514) produced the first known image of Munich, a famous woodcut of the city 'from the east'. Surrounded by a city wall with 110 towers and a raging river Isar containing several transportation floats, the dome-less towers of the Frauenkirche soar above the clearly identifiable St Peter's church and the rest of the numerous buildings of this still relatively young and still very much medium-sized settlement.

Though Munich was now an established royal residence city of rising affluence, with concomitant splendid buildings and works of art, Bavaria still was not home to an elector of the Holy Roman Empire, and it did not have much political influence outside its own borders. Indicative of the provincial nature of the Munich court is that just 164 people attended to Duke Sigmund's royal court in 1465, miniscule compared with the around 5,000 people available to Bavaria's Elector Karl Theodor in 1781. In order to realise its aim of becoming a bigger player in the corridors of European power-brokering, Bavaria would have to consolidate and unify. Once Bavarian unification was complete, with power emanating from its central core of Munich, Bavaria would typically spend the next few centuries striving to either hold what influence it had in a world increasingly shaped by great powers, such as Austria, France, Britain and Spain, or find alliances that would give it a greater say than its medium size seemed to warrant.

Landshut War of Succession

The 1504-1505 Landshut War of Succession was in effect a civil war between the elector of the Palatinate on the Rhine, land not contiguous with Bavaria, though ruled by a line of the Wittelsbach family, and the Munich-based Upper Bavarian Wittelsbach line. It was sparked by the death in 1503 of Georg der Reiche ('the Rich'; 1479-1503), the last duke of Lower Bavaria, and it concerned who should be his successor. It culminated in victory for Upper Bavaria and Bavarian unification, meaning from 1505 Munich's 13,447 inhabitants now resided in Bavaria's primary capital and now only royal residence city.

In the wake of the war, Duke Albrecht IV der Weise ('the Wise'; 1447-1508) decreed on 8 July 1506 that Bavaria was henceforth indivisible and the first-born son in the male line would immutably inherit the entire dukedom, signifying, in theory, another building block in the construction of a considerably more influential Bavaria. On Albrecht's death in 1508, Duke Wilhelm IV (1493-1550) took the throne in Munich, but against the explicit wishes of his father, he ruled jointly (in reasonable harmony) with Ludwig X (1495-1545), his art-loving brother, today most famous for the glorious Lower Bavarian court he had built in Landshut and his passionate promotion of the Renaissance. Real power, however, firmly resided in Munich, reflected in a growing court that grew in personnel from 485 people in 1508 to 866 by 1571, financed primarily by the city's tax-paying citizens. Munich was still ostensibly governed by 12 members of the Inner Council, led by the mayor, and 24 members of the Outer Council. Although dukes theoretically were not to have much influence on the politics

Suffused with intricate details, Jacob Sandtner's wooden model of Munich provides a comprehensive view of the architecture and layout of the city in the 16th and 17th centuries

of Munich, the reality of the royal court being in the city meant that regardless of which duke reigned he interfered as much as was deemed necessary.

The growing importance of Munich as *the* centre of power in Bavaria was also reflected in a stream of influential visitors, most important of whom was Holy Roman Emperor Charles V (1500-1558) in June 1530 on his way to the Reichstag in Augsburg from his coronation by the Pope in Bologna. Munich's population turned out in huge numbers to see the new emperor, members of his court, various Papal representatives and around 300 members of the Empire's nobility. Charles V stayed in the Neuvest, celebrated mass in the Frauenkirche and was honoured with a meal consisting of an impressive 32 courses.

By 1580, Munich's population had grown to around 20,000 and the city had a total of 1,265 buildings, reflecting the medium scale of the city at this time.

Munich, now around 400 years old, was no longer a young settlement, and with age came a greater degree of sophistication. The 16th century was hugely significant in the later establishment of Munich as something approaching a *Kunststadt*, or a 'city of art'. Duke Albrecht V's (1528-1579) 1567-completed Kunstkammer (a kind of art depository and museum), for example, which later served as the city mint and today as the Landesamt für Denkmalpflege (Land Bureau for the Conservation of Historic Monuments), is one of southern Germany's best examples of Renaissance architecture. And in 1571, the Antiquarian (Antiquarium), with superb depictions of Bavarian cities and countless antique figurines, was completed. But this attempt at defining itself as a city of high-class art engendered the parallel problem of huge debt, something that was to hinder the city's development for centuries.

One of the city's most important works of art in this period has proved to be a fascination to modern historians and a valuable source of information on the layout and gothic style of Munich at the end of the Middle Ages. Taking around six years to create, in 1570 Jacob Sandtner finished his wooden model of the city for Albrecht V (who also commissioned similar models for Bavaria's other major cities), which is now on display at the Bayerisches Nationalmuseum (Bavarian National Museum). Periodically updated for around a century, notably with the addition of the Residenz and the huge Jesuit College, the model clearly shows the first impression travellers would have had approaching this ostentatiously gothic city: a vast wall encircling the city, interspersed by a series of keep-like structures and the distant but ever-impressive Frauenkirche towers, now topped by their characteristic cupolas. On entering the city through one of the huge gates, little narrow passages and side streets would have revealed themselves, and as visitors made their way to the city centre through the relatively wide main streets to the bustling and noisy Markplatz they might have spotted trees in gardens, the gables and eaves on the houses, and most certainly a number of churches, though perhaps not the numerous hidden courtyards. Indeed, Munich was becoming increasingly a city noted for its architecture and style. One contemporary scribe, Quad von Kinkelbachs, recorded: 'Above all other German cities, Munich ... has a beauty of the highest order ... [as well as] greatness, beauty and cleanliness.'

Up until the 15th century, brick constructions in the city were reserved primarily for churches and other significant buildings. But the proliferation of major fires, mostly significantly in 1418 and in 1429, propelled the city council to further intensify the production of bricks. In addition to, and building on, the 1327 building regulations, a series of further edicts were drawn up, culminating in the 44 articles of the 1489 *stat München – pau-sartz und -ordnung*, which *inter alia* regulated buildings in regard to fire safety, their effect on neighbouring buildings and even the design of fireplaces in buildings.

Centre of the Counter-Reformation

When, on the eve of All Saints' Day of 13 October 1517, a monk and theologian by the name of Martin Luther (1483-1546) pinned his 95 Theses criticising abuses in the Catholic Church, particularly the sale of indulgences, to the door of the main church in Wittenberg (a common practice to provoke public debate), he could never have imagined that it would set off a chain of events that would reverberate across the Continent, destroy the façade of religious and cultural unity of Christendom in Europe and herald in what is now called the Reformation. For a variety of reasons, both secular and religious, the period encompassing the European Reformation saw, for example, Henry VIII replace the Pope as head of the church in England and the Holy Roman Empire go through contortions that seemed destined to tear it apart. In the middle of this was a dispute between rulers who loosely followed Luther or some other form of 'Protestantism' and those who aimed to remain steadfast in their defence of Catholicism.

Luther's teachings, disseminated by preachers and other followers in numerous speeches and leaflets, facilitated by Johannes Gensfleisch zum Gutenberg's (c.1397-1468) revolutionary printing press, found a significant though minority of followers in Munich. In fact, Bavaria's Duke Wilhelm IV appeared to see the possibility of Luther as a force for good in the much-needed fight to reform the abuses of the Catholic Church. This radically altered when Luther was found guilty of heresy at his trial at Worms, confirming the *Bull Exsurge Dominine*, which forbade any help to Luther and ordered the burning of all his writings within the Empire. Rulers now split loosely between pro- and anti-Lutheranism, with Wilhelm siding decisively with Catholicism. The beheading in 1523 of a bakery worker – on the orders of Wilhelm – for being a follower of Luther provided a foretaste of what the future held. On 6 January 1528, 29 'newly baptised' Münchners, including three women, were arrested and tortured. Nine refused to repent and were executed: six men were killed by burning and three women were condemned to the same fate until, in an act of 'mercy', they were drowned in the Isar, then burned. The duke, however, was more lenient with the city's patricians who had Protestant leanings than with the general populace. For example, the wealthy Bernhard Dichtl's punishment for appearing to be sympathetic to Lutheranism was just two and a half weeks' jail and a fine of 1,000 gulden.

A second surge of Protestantism in the city accompanied the accession in 1550 of the seemingly more enlightened Duke Albrecht V. This façade of tolerance was soon swept away, and in 1558 he withdrew Protestant-influenced reforms, thus, heralding in a further period of repression. On 18 January 1558, Albrecht ordered representatives of the city council to explain why bookshops were still selling 'heretic' books, 'paintings, letters and figures' and why the council had done nothing about it. Consequently, he ordered a search of numerous shops and demanded heavier censorship of Protestant works. Further decrees ruled that only Catholics could be citizens of the city, with the obvious effect of prohibiting city officials from following Protestantism, and he ordered that members of the city council who followed Luther's teachings had one month to leave Munich. A total of 46 people did just that, and though it represented a tiny per cent of the city's population, it comprised some of the wealthiest, most highly educated and most influential citizens. At the same time as the city was losing some of its elite, in 1559 it gained the ultra-religious Jesuits and with them the label as the Counter-Reformation, pro-Catholic capital of the Empire.

Munich soon came to identify itself with religion in a manner never before experienced in the city. Catholic conformism was the order of the day, and the overweening piety of the Jesuits manifested itself to Munich's population in the requirement to perform daily prayers and to attend regular confession and communion; in the building of magnificent churches; and in new music and religious festivals, including innumerable processions through the city, to celebrate Corpus Christi and Good Friday, for example. In addition, many of Munich's future elite were now educated at the new Jesuit college, part of a vast complex of Jesuit buildings, including the extant and still impressive St Michael's Church on Neuhauser Straße, the biggest, and to many admirers, the most impressive late-Renaissance church in Germany. Just as interesting, however, was that an estimated 15 to 20 per cent of Jesuit students across the city were not from the patrician class but from ordinary working families.

The financial cost of defending Catholicism, exemplified in the construction of such symbolic buildings as the Jesuit complex, or taking the fight abroad, most notably in a war in Cologne, was ruinously expensive and Bavaria and particularly its capital city suffered as a result. It did not help that Wilhelm V (1548-1626) abolished the city's salt monopoly in 1587 in favour of – in essence – a similar one for himself. Perhaps, however, thriftiness could hardly have been expected of Wilhelm V: for his wedding to Princess Renata von Lothringen in 1566, his father, Albrecht V, had persuaded the Bavarian government to find the exorbitant sum of 100,000 gulden for the celebrations, today remembered in the Munich Rathaus Glockenspiel. By 1593 Bavaria had a colossal debt of 4.8 million gulden, compared with an annual income of just 300,000 gulden, and this played a major role in persuading Wilhelm V to abdicate in 1598 in favour of his eldest surviving son, Duke Maximilian I (1573-1651). But rather than enter a period of much-needed calm, Munich – in fact, much of the Holy Roman Empire – was on the edge of a precipice. Ahead stood the Thirty Years War, and for Munich, foreign occupation and a duke who seemed to be eternally fighting or fleeing.

Maximilian I was something of a 'man of action', more of an adventurer than any other Bavarian ruler up to this point. Nevertheless, in keeping with his education under strict Jesuit tutelage, he was extremely religious, saw hard work as a godly virtue, and for good measure he spoke fluent Latin, French, Italian, Czech and some Spanish. Maximilian's reign mirrored the wider trend towards the diminution of powers away from the Holy Roman Empire in favour of territorial rulers, and within Bavaria, favour at the Munich court became one of the few ways in which cities, the church and members of the nobility could exert substantial influence. Moreover, Maximilian attempted to bring some kind of order to the mountain of debt he had inherited. He nationalised the Weißbier brewing industry and erected his own breweries (including one in 1606 at Platzl, today the location of the tourist-loving Hofbräuhaus), providing himself with a huge source of revenue.

And in contrast to the ever-more luxurious and palatial surroundings of the duke and his court, Munich's population (by 1600 numbering around 20,000) was put under increasing surveillance, pressured into ever-greater piety and other forms of social control, and was soon faced with foreign occupation.

Indeed, political manoeuvring from his base in Munich was never enough for Maximilian. Characterised as a typical 'absolutist' ruler, he was enthralled by the notion of Bavaria becoming a regional power of renown, which motivated him to start building a grand Residenz in Munich, adjacent to the site of the Neuveste: the Hofkapelle (Chapel Court) was finished in 1601, Reiche Kapelle (Rich Chapel) in 1607 and Kaisersaal (Imperial Hall) between 1612 and 1616, originally decorated with paintings and tapestries by Peter Candid (1548-1628) and ceiling paintings by Italian Andrea Michieli (1539-1614). The biggest building project, though, was a new city wall, which was started in 1619, a year after the outbreak of the Thirty Years War, and as time proved, not nearly early enough to withstand even the threat of an attack.

It was also under Maximilian I in the early 1600s that the apogee of Jesuit education was reached when the likes of Jakob Bidermann, Jeremias Drexel and Jacob Balde helped Munich become a renowned European centre of Jesuit literature and poetry as well as of Jesuit theatrical and musical productions. Such plays inevitably imparted a sense of Jesuit-inspired morality and modesty, and stressed the value of hard work. Similarly, by 1609 city officials were under orders from Maximilian to order the arrest of any Münchner caught going to the pub instead of attending mass. In the same year, a leather worker was locked up in the tower for working on a Sunday, after which he was ordered on a pilgrimage to nearby Ramersdorf. If adhering to strict religious observation was not enough, an expanding population added to bad harvests in the second half of the 16th century led to a substantial rise in the price of many staple foods to beyond anything workers could afford, exacerbating the general discontent of the city's population. In a period, therefore, when life in Munich was becoming increasingly tightly controlled by religious zealots and when food supplies were intermittently precarious, the population became caught up in the Empire's power and religious disputes.

By 1609, Protestantism had gathered into union around the Wittelsbach elector of the Palatinate, Friedrich IV (1574-1610), and Catholics had joined together in the Catholic League, centred in Munich and led by the Wittelsbach duke of Bavaria, Maximilian I. There was no inevitability about the outbreak of the Thirty Years War (1618-1648) and religion, though central, was only one of a number of causes. The initial military successes of the Catholic League brought great prestige to Maximilian's court in Munich as he led the re-Catholicisation of Austria and Bohemia. The reward from the emperor was an electorship for Bavaria (originally taken from the Palatinate but a new Palatine electoral seat was created at the end of the war) in 1623, meaning an all-important vote on future emperors, an honour that had eluded Bavarian rulers for centuries.

But while Maximilian's military and political skills seemed to have succeeded where others had failed, for Munich's population there was a further tightening of state control. The high inflation of the splendidly named 'Kipper- und Wipperzeit' resulted in sparse supplies of affordable basic foods and textiles. To make matters worse, 1627 was an extremely cold year, with snow in June, while further bad weather led to crop failures in 1628, which magnified the sense of crisis in a year when the city was also attempting to cope with another attack of the plague. Further strains on the city's finances arrived with the rebuilding and strengthening of the city's defences, still unfinished when the city was threatened with occupation by King Gustav Adolf of Sweden (1594-1632) in 1631. The previously all-conquering Maximilian fled the capital with his court, and with Munich's defeat inevitable, the population agreed to a deal with the Swedes: the city would be handed over without a fight, while King Gustav promised to uphold Catholicism, respect private property and prevent burning and pillaging, all in exchange for the impossibly high sum of 450,000 gulden. The agreement meant that the people of Munich were living under

Ratskeller
S
U

and most importantly he lusted after power and glory. Similar to subsequent Bavarian leaders, he had to decide whether to support one of the two great continental European powers: France or Austria. In 1683, Max Emanuel's 11,300 Bavarian troops helped the Holy Roman Empire's forces push back a 200,000-strong Turkish army threatening Vienna, and in September 1684, as leader of the Empire's forces, he ensured his 14,000 troops played a significant role in again fighting the Turks, before further enhancing his prestige in 1688 by leading the conquest of Belgrade. Turkish prisoners from his campaigns played a significant role in building a canal network – albeit never completed – from Munich to palaces outside the city centre, including the newly built Lustheim and Schleißheim, both symbolic of a shift to a French rather than Italian cultural influence. Turkish servants – captured during the wars – soon became the fashion amongst Munich patrician families, while legacies of Max Emanuel's reign are apparent in contemporary Munich street names such as Türkenstraße, Kurfürstenstraße and Belgradstraße.

In the Nine Years War (or War of the Palatine Succession, 1688-1697), Max Emanuel sided against France and joined the victorious Grand Alliance (which included England and Spain), for which he was handed the governorship of the Spanish Netherlands (today Belgium and Luxembourg). Consequently, in 1692 the ever-ambitious Max transferred his court to Brussels, leaving Munich no longer a *Residenzstadt* (royal capital city), a loss that hugely exacerbated the city's economic difficulties.

Massacre at Sendling

Max Emanuel's visions of greater glory and power had hardly got off the ground when the death in 1700 of King Charles II of Spain sparked the War of the Spanish Succession (1701-1714), which again embroiled Europe's major powers. Moving his court back to Munich, this time he opted for the side of France, whose coalition was finally defeated in 1714 by the Duke of Marlborough's forces of Britain, Austria and the Netherlands. This, however, was not before Austrian occupation troops had exacted a terrible price on the people of Munich in what became known as *Mordweihnacht*, or 'Christmas Massacre'.

From around October 1705, a sizeable collection of little more than farmers from Upper and Lower Bavaria headed towards Munich with the intent of ridding their home of its Austrian occupiers. Their call to arms was: 'Better to die Bavarian than perish with the nonsense of emperors.' Poorly trained, even more poorly armed (possibly only a third had any weapons), and picking up volunteers as they marched, more than 3,000 reached the outskirts of Munich on 24 December to face Austria's soldiers. At around 10 o'clock in the evening they reached Thalkirchen, then Sendling, and arrived just outside the city at Angertor. Unable to force their way into the city, they headed for Isartor, only to be beaten back. Subsequently, the experienced Austrian soldiers managed to surround the Bavarians, who panicked and in the chaos attempted to flee. Most reached Sendling before coming under further attack, resulting in the massacre of more than 2,000 people in front of the city gates while as many as 750 prisoners were left to freeze or bleed to death.

Mass burials took place between 26 and 31 December, and in memory of the slain an enormous mural was painted on an outer wall of the Sendling Church. It took considerably longer for bitter memories of the slaughter of *Mordweihnacht* to recede; instead, for many decades the events of Christmas 1705 manifested within Bavarians a deep-felt bitterness and distrust against Austrians.

Though heavily indebted and war weary, by 1715 the city had somehow found the wherewithal and the finance to build the Dreifaltigkeitskirche (a church on today's Promenadeplatz) and the Bürgersaal (another church, on today's Neuhauser Straße). In the course of the War of the Spanish Succession, Max Emanuel, lost his title as elector and also his territory, before having both returned at the war's end. Undaunted by the total collapse of the city's finances, in addition to already lavishing Munich with two glorious churches, he continued to patronise various art projects and hold extravagant celebrations, including paying four million gulden, the equivalent of a whole year's income of the electorate of Bavaria, to fund the wedding of his son to Maria Amalia (1701-1756), the second daughter of the by now dead Emperor Joseph I.

It has been estimated that Bavaria's debt corresponded to around 700 per cent of its yearly income, so when Max Emanuel died in 1726 Munich's population might have been forgiven for breathing a collective sigh of relief. Instead, however, the city celebrated its ambitious and cavalier elector for raising Bavaria's profile and prestige across Europe, while he was credited with Munich being widely admired as a one of Europe's rising centres of art. This contin-

The original Cuvilliés Theater was built between 1751 and 1755 and was considered a 'jewel of the rococo'

ued under Max Emanuel's successor, Karl Albrecht (1697-1745), as Munich became a European centre for rococo art and architecture. Among a host of other artists, the Asam brothers, Cosmas Damian (1686-1739) and Egid Quirin (1692-1750), plus Georg Desamarées (1697-1776), Johan Baptist Zimmermann (1680-1758), Johan Baptist Straub (1704-1784) and most famously François Cuvilliés the Elder (1695-1768) all played leading roles in various art and architecture projects. Rococo installations of European-wide significance were the Reiche Zimmer (Rich Rooms) and the Cuvilliés Theater in the Residenz, work on the palace at Nymphenburg and nearby mini-palace of Amalienburg, the Asamkirche St Johann Nepomuk in Sendlinger Straße and even the city's oldest church, St Peter's, was given a rococo renovation.

Karl Albrecht's foreign policy was based on the fundamental tenet of neutrality whenever possible, and this – perhaps slightly paradoxically, though very much welcomed – led to his being elected Emperor of the Holy Roman Empire in 1742, four centuries after Ludwig IV had become the only previous Munich-Wittelsbach to hold this exalted office. This meant that once again

Munich was a focal point of the Holy Roman Empire, once again caught in the crossfire of great power politics, and again occupied by the still despised Austrians, who were far from forgiven for the infamous *Mordweihnacht* massacre of almost four decades earlier. The Austrians were driven out of the city in 1744, but Emperor Karl VII's sudden death in 1745 brought Munich's rather ignominious period as home of the emperor to an abrupt end.

Many accounts describe the accession of Max III Joseph (1727-1777), Bavaria's new elector, as a *Glücksfall*, or 'stroke of luck'. The new elector, heavily influenced by the development throughout Europe of Enlightenment thought, secured peace with Austria in 1745 and concentrated on mild church reforms (including the abolition of the Jesuit Orders) and set about drastically reducing the enormous 32-million-gulden mountain of debt. Significant achievements of Max Joseph's reign included the establishment of the Bavarian Academy of Science in 1759, the codification of Bavarian law in Wiguläus Freiherr von Kreittmayr's *Codex Maximilianeus* of 1756, the modernisation of criminal and civil law and court procedures, plus the introduction of compulsory schooling in 1771.

Regardless of this 'Age of Enlightenment', religion still played a significant role in the life of Munich's population, highlighted by 4,000 members of the Maria Men's Congregation gathering for the 1751 Whitsun pilgrimage from St Michael's Church in Munich to Freising, around 40 kilometres north. Nevertheless, cultural activities had been decisively loosened from the hem of the now considerably less dominant Catholic Church. In addition, Munich was by this time an established cultural centre of some significance and in 1762 attracted members of the Mozart family, including the six-year-old Wolfgang Amadeus (1756-1791). Moreover, the young Mozart and his family lived on Frauenplatz 4 from 7 December 1774 to 6 March 1775, and in January 1775 Mozart's opera *La finta gardiniera* premiered in the presence of Max Joseph at the theatre on Salvatorplatz. Famously, Mozart offered his services to the elector but was turned down on account of there not being a position available at the time.

Furthermore, in these more enlightened times, Max Joseph tolerated increasing numbers of Protestants in the city, though they were still without citizenship rights and were prohibited

Right: though by the mid-18th century, St Michael's was no longer a Jesuit stronghold, Catholicism still played a considerable role in the lives of Münchners

from acquiring property. Similarly, the ban on visits by Jews to the city was abolished, as was the ban on Jews trading, and by 1750, Munich was home to 20 Jews.

On Max Joseph's death in 1777, the city's sadness for a much-loved ruler was palpable, hardly surprising when one contrasts his peaceful reign with the chaos, debt and occupation of many of his predecessors. With no heir, he was succeeded by a 'foreigner': Karl Theodor (1724-1799), elector of the Palatinate-Sulzbach line, a Wittelsbach, a Catholic and spectacularly unpopular with it.

An American-Englishman

Just inside the English Garden, a leisurely stroll from Munich's Altstadt, past the Residenz and Hofgarten, a few hundred metres away from Haus der Kunst (House of Art) on Prinzregentenstraße, stands a monument to a Count Rumford (1753-1814). Today, in Britain at least, if Rumford is known at all, he is remembered as the founder of the Royal Institution, the oldest independent science research institute in the world, which recently described him as a: 'former soldier and statesman, he was by all accounts, ruthless and arrogant, callously cunning and devious, an unprincipled spy and a calculating womaniser; but he was also a philanthropist, a brilliantly effective social reformer, an ingenious inventor and an exceptionally innovative scientist.'

The later Lord Rumford was born Benjamin Thompson on 26 March 1753 in Woburn, Massachusetts, in America, at the time still a British colony, to a farmer father and an army officer's daughter. His marriage to a rich widow in November 1772 transformed him from a schoolteacher with limited prospects into a member of the landed gentry. On the outbreak of the American War of Independence he sided with the British, for whom he possibly worked as a spy, before he joined thousands of other British soldiers evacuated from Boston on 17 March 1776, eventually landing in London some time in April.

Typical for Thompson, he manoeuvred himself into a position where he could meet influential people and was handed a 100-pound-a-year non-existent post in the 'Province of Georgia'. He seems to have spent the time experimenting with gunpowder and in 1781 published his findings as *New Experiments Upon Gunpowder*, which foresaw his later work as one of Europe's foremost scientific thinkers.

A foray back to America to fight for the British was followed by a return to Europe (including sitting for the great British portrait painter Thomas Gainsborough in 1783) in order to visit Continental Europe, where in Strasbourg he met Prince Maximilian, a Palatine Wittelsbach, who later became elector of Bavaria and then the country's first king. With a letter of introduction from Maximilian, Thompson set off for Munich, where, in characteristic Thompson style, he soon became the personal confidant and fixer for Bavaria's Karl Theodor, and arguably the most influential Anglo-Saxon in Munich's 850-year history. On seeking permission from Britain's King George III (who was also elector of Hanover) to work for the Bavarian royal family, which was granted, he was also – for reasons not altogether clear – awarded a knighthood. It is possible that Thompson had agreed to continue spying for the British, who at the time were hopeful that Bavarian foreign policy would not favour France, Britain's main European adversary.

Max Joseph's death without an heir in 1777 had resulted in the disappearance of the rump-Bavaria Wittelsbach line. The subsequent accession of Karl Theodor, a Wittelsbach elector from the much more enlightened Bavarian Palat inate line of Neuberg-Sulzbach, unified rump Bavaria with the Palatinate. But the new elector's reign started in a less than auspicious vein when he made it patently obvious that he was moving himself and his court from Mannheim on the river Rhine to Munich with extreme reluctance. Moreover, by taking his huge Mannheim entourage with him (including court artists and musicians, this amounted to around 3,000 people), who all needed to be housed, he offended the Munich court and the population of an already over-crowded city. Indeed, he seems to have been so enamoured with his new Bavarian acquisition that he made numerous attempts to swap it for the Austrian-controlled Netherlands, failing only due to the opposition of the increasingly powerful Prussian state, led by Frederick the Great (1712-1786). For such 'treachery', Karl Theodor was never forgiven and – in the eyes of the population – it tainted absolutely everything else he tried to achieve.

In contrast to earlier accounts, however, and regardless of the obvious enmity the people of Munich had for him, historians now paint a more positive picture of Karl Theodor's reign. He did, after all, invite Mozart to compose an opera for him, which, under the title *Idomeneo*, premiered on 29 January 1781 at the Cuvilliés Theater in the Residenz. Furthermore, he had 2,000 paint-

Sir Benjamin Thompson warming himself on one of his own 'Rumford Stoves', as depicted by the great 18th-century British caricaturist James Gillray

Reform and Constitution

In 1781, there were 20 cloisters or religious communities living in the city of Munich, including 686 monks and nuns, totalling around 1.9 per cent of the approximately 37,000 inhabitants. But religious structures of one sort or another accounted for somewhere in the region of 20 to 25 per cent of the city's buildings. Though considerably weakened since the high point of Jesuit-designed piety of the 17th century, these religious orders still held considerable influence in this almost exclusively Catholic city. Under Enlightenment influence, however, Munich joined many other parts of Europe in secularisation. The dissolution of the cloisters – primarily in 1803 – under the guidance of Montgelas occurred in Munich with surprisingly little opposition from the city's population. But secularisation entailed far more than merely closing down buildings and dispersing religious orders. It also encompassed the collection of countless valuable works of art, many of European significance, as well as books and documents, the majority of which were delivered to Munich's central archive and libraries from across the entire Bavarian region, and they were soon joined by treasures from former independent cities such as Freising, Regensburg, Passau, Nuremberg and Augsburg.

Similar to the popular attitude towards the cloisters, it is interesting to note that the destruction of historic buildings, such as the Franciscan cloister, did not evoke the same anger as when some traditional religious processions were prohibited, and more pertinently when religious holidays were scrapped, with one Munich protest resulting in the arrest of 167 people.

Secularisation also entailed lifting the ban on exclusive citizenship rights for Catholics in towns, cities and villages across Bavaria, including the all-Catholic Munich, particularly relevant as Elector Max Joseph's wife was Protestant. Moreover, a cleverly ambiguous change of Bavarian law signed by the elector at Amberg proved to have a fundamental impact in changing the character of the Munich population. The law decreed that Catholicism would no longer be a prerequisite for settlement rights, though it was unspecific about exactly where in Bavaria the law was applicable. It soon transpired that it was implementable across the whole state, and it was this which enabled a Protestant mass to take place in the city on 6 April 1800 in the Residenz, the first since Gustav Adolf and his Swedish army had occupied the city in 1632.

But most Münchners remained unconvinced by any suggestion of a thawing in the relationship between Catholicism and other religions. In 1801, for example, with many Protestants already employed in Karl Theodor's administration, Max Joseph had to threaten an extremely reluctant Munich city council with severe punishment if it continued to equivocate and did not immediately approve citizenship for the Mannheim Protestant businessman Johann Balthasar Michel. The elector even threatened to jail the council if members employed any further delaying tactics, until, at the considerable cost of 470 gulden, Michel became the first Protestant citizen of Munich since 1569. Though genuine anti-Protestant feeling still ran deep in the Munich population, it did not deter some 6,000 non-Catholics from taking up citizenship of the city by 1826, around nine per cent of the around 65,000 population. By 1798, around 200 Jews were living in the city, but, as in much of Europe, Jews still had fewer rights than most other people, and it was only in 1813 that they legally received trading and political rights across the whole of Bavaria. With prejudices against Jews still prevalent, and bearing in mind they had been 'officially' banned from the city since 1442, by 1825 the Jewish population of the city had risen to a modest 607 and by 1840 to 1,432.

As well as preaching religious tolerance, Montgelas's secularisation had a more practical effect: it has been posited that without the enormous income the state received from secularisation, Bavaria's huge debt (which rose from 15 million to 80 million gulden between 1799 and 1806/7) could conceivably have led to the collapse of the state rather than witness its march – albeit a stuttering one – to modernity.

The path to reform was far from a linear process, and it was particularly complicated in the wider context of Bavaria's relationship with France, now led by Napoleon Bonaparte, and in the process of dominating wide tracts of the European Continent. Neutrality, along with receiving secret subventions from the British that were intended to keep France away from a Bavarian alliance, had seemed enough to keep Max Joseph's new state out of trouble. However, after spending years since the French Revolution attempting to steer a path between France and Austria (prompted by fears of being swallowed by Austria and memories of the massacre of 1705), expediency meant that in August 1805 Bavaria joined a military alliance with what

Right: Maximilian I, Bavaria's first king

OEUVRES
DE
BUFON

seemed to be the side of the victor, France. On the tailcoats of Emperor Napoleon, therefore, who appeared to be something approaching a political and military genius, Bavaria seemed destined to be on the right side of history, in the process gaining the prestige and influence it had coveted for centuries. The situation, as usual, looked slightly different from Munich. Occupied by Austrian troops between 13 September and 12 October 1805, the city – as it had on so many occasions – also had to quarter countless processions of foreign troops. The situation seemed to have improved when a France-led alliance defeated Austria on 20 October 1805, particularly when four days later at 7 o'clock in the evening Napoleon Bonaparte and his entourage entered Munich through Karlstor to the ringing of bells and to the jubilation of an enthusiastic population. The procession went through Neuhausertor, along Kaufingergasse to Marienplatz, before turning left to the Residenz, where Napoleon stayed overnight.

The alliance appeared to have handsomely paid off for Max Joseph when on 2 December Bavarian troops helped defeat Austria at Austerlitz, resulting in territorial gains for Bavaria. Even more so when on 1 January 1806 it was announced in Munich by royal herald – again to bells, plus gunfire and trumpets followed by a short celebration in the Residenz – that Bavaria was to be raised to a kingdom and Max Joseph raised from elector to king, all by the grace of Emperor Napoleon. The pay-off for Napoleon was Bavarian troops, and lots of them, and in order to further knit Bavaria and France closer together, Bavaria was compelled to join Napoleon's Confederation of the Rhine (with a further 15 states) while in 1806 Max Joseph's eldest daughter was married off to Napoleon's stepson, Eugène de Beauharnais. In April 1809, Munich was again occupied by Austrian troops, who withdrew later in the month after Napoleon's troops again rode to the rescue.

In 1810, many of Munich's long-suffering population (now at 48,000) turned out to celebrate crown prince Ludwig's wedding to Princess Therese von Sachsen-Hildburghausen, not far from an area known as the Sendlinger Berg, with horse racing and other festivities. Repeated since on an almost yearly basis, in its early decades the festival became partly a propaganda event with the overt aim of binding together new and old Bavarians from all corners of the expanded realm at a recognisable national Bavarian event. Under the name of Oktoberfest, it is today the world's largest festival of its kind.

Napoleon Bonarparte's grand 1805 entrance into Munich, as conveyed by Nicolas-Antoine Taunay, 1808

This wedding apart, the city had little reason to celebrate over the next few years. War and occupation were taking their toll, as was Napoleon's economic blockade of Britain, which had provided trade, particularly finished goods, with the Continent. Murmurings of discontent increased in volume. The loss of around 30,000 out of a Bavarian force of around 36,000 in Napoleon's catastrophic 1812 Russia campaign hardened the capital against the alliance with France. Further military defeats and the loss of more Bavarian soldiers meant many in Munich who had once greeted Napoleon as a saviour now saw him as a shortcut to further disaster. Switching sides to join the anti-French alliance comprising the major powers of Britain and Austria, plus the fast-rising power of Prussia, was not inevitable, but it was Bavaria's best hope. Bavarian troops could count themselves on the side of the victors when Napoleon was decisively defeated at Leipzig in 1813, and then conclusively at Waterloo in 1815. By 1808, Montgelas had managed to push through a host of Bavaria-wide reforms, including a first written constitution, and the population had been handed fundamental rights, such as protection of private property, freedom of speech and freedom to practise religion, vital in light of the mixed confessions of the populations in the newly acquired territories of Franconia and Swabia. The 'revolution from above' may have been multifaceted and uneven but it fundamentally altered Munich. By 1804, sweeping reform of the city administration had, in effect, removed the Inner and Outer councils, which had been in existence since 1304; in its place was a unified council comprised of 12 councillors (including two mayors) plus 12 business or trade representatives. Even the monk in the city's coat of arms had to make way for a king's crown, a lion and an 'M' for Maximilian. Though some of these reforms were transitory, altered after Montgelas fell out of favour, in their totality they represented a telling shift of power away from a local to a state level.

Moreover, the insipient construction of a more centralised and bureaucratic state required the Bavarian capital to find and train a number of educated civil servants, while the 1807-reorganised Bavarian Academy of Science needed to attract talent from across Germany, a move less than popular in Munich. As pointed out by Richard Bauer, the Munich population seemed to have had 'a traditional antipathy towards foreigners that in combination with old confessional prejudices and envy of the preferential treatment of new Münchners in public office and privileged jobs … rose to bare hatred.' The other side of this was an apparent 'know-it-all' attitude and 'overbearing arrogance' from these so-called Nordlichter (Northern Lights), producing an antagonism which occasionally escalated into violent confrontations between Münchners and 'foreigners'. In the medium term, while implanting in many Münchners a high degree of suspicion of northerners, it opened a door that was to have a significant impact in the following decades. Indeed, the city became a magnet for 'foreigners', notably in the sciences but more importantly in the world of art. In fact, during the next 100 years, Munich rose steadily to become Germany's outstanding art capital and one of the most renowned in Europe, attracting star names from far and wide. The role Max Joseph's successor, King Ludwig I (1786-1868), played in that dramatic rise was immense.

Chapter 3

CAPITAL OF ART TO CAPITAL OF THE MOVEMENT (1815-1945)

~

Athens on the Isar

'This is All Souls Day,' recorded Anna Mary Howitt on 1 November 1850.

> The principal cemetery is illuminated and decorated with flowers, girlands and various devices, and all Munich goes out to see it. We had heard of this grand day for weeks, and therefore were rather curious about it. We set off at two o'clock, and on our way through the Türken Strasse met King Ludwig walking alone. Spite of all the old king's failings my heart warms to him as the generous and noble patron of art; and as I made him a low reverence as he passed, and received a gracious smile and bow.

Howitt, from Britain, was studying art in Munich, and though she did not leave a legacy of great paintings, in her *An Art-Student in Munich* she wrote an at times beautifully illuminating account of her time in the city, It seems odd today, but being passed in a Munich street by King Ludwig was not so unusual at that time, as other written accounts bear witness. Title aside, he was, after all, no longer king of Bavaria. Revolution by way of an Irish-cum-Spanish dancer had seen to that.

By the time Ludwig succeeded to the Bavarian throne in 1825, even though there had been some minor reversals of reforms, Montgelas had been able to lay the basis of a modern bureaucratised and more centralised state. He had fallen out of favour soon after Napoleon's defeat, and Ludwig had little interest in further moulding a state on the French model. Indeed, Ludwig greatly disliked Montgelas and much that he stood for, and he had little enthusiasm for allowing the egalitarian ideals of the French Revolution to hinder his autocratic style of kingship. If Montgelas had been more concerned with constructing a modern

Right: King Ludwig I was largely responsible for raising Munich's reputation to one of Europe's most impressive centres of art

state apparatus, Ludwig was primarily interested in – aside from beautiful women – building a capital fit for a king, and in the process of doing so he radically altered the Munich cityscape. 'I will make Munich a city that everybody who wants to know Germany must know,' he is famously quoted as saying. His legacy is a series of buildings, sculptures, statues and works of art that led to Munich becoming known across Europe, with more than a hint of hyperbole, as 'Athens on the Isar'. Indeed, the antiquity-obsessed Ludwig somehow engineered things – albeit with the acquiescence of Britain, France and Russia – so that in 1832 his son Otto could become the first king of the newly independent Greece.

The neo-classical art and architecture Ludwig promoted in Munich is exemplified by Leo von Klenze's (1784-1864) Glyptothek and Propyläen, and Georg Friedrich Ziebland's (1800–1873) Antikensammlung, all three at Königsplatz, the centre of Ludwig's homage to antiquity. The king's aim, however, was not merely aesthetic. Rather than rely on traditional power politics, he believed that without a glorious capital, Bavaria could hardly be expected to be taken seriously in its aim of becoming a more substantial European power. He was fortunate in his quest in that he was able to call upon outstanding architects with a similar mindset, most famously Klenze and Friedrich von Gärtner (1791-1847). Ludwigstraße – part of the Maxvorstadt city extension, with its grand buildings and imposing boulevard-like appearance, leading from the Feldherrnhalle (modelled on the Loggia dei Lanzi in Florence) at Odeonsplatz to Siegestor (modelled on a Roman triumphal arch) – was also primarily the creation of both Klenze and Gärtner. Anna Mary Howitt witnessed the 1850 opening of Siegestor:

> The great festivities were terminated today with the opening of the Siegesthor, or Triumphal Arch, at the end of the beautiful Ludwig Strasse … [I]t is constructed of stone brought across from the neighbourhood of Regensburg, and is embellished with medallions and basso-relieves … executed in white marble from Carrara and the Tyrol. The masonry is said to surpass in solidity and beauty anything in Europe … This Triumphal Arch, as may be imagined, forms a striking termination to the noble Ludwig Strasse, and a most impressive entrance to Munich.

Which is, one would guess, precisely the reaction Ludwig hoped for.

During the 19th-century Munich became one of the first cities in Europe to draw up a comprehensive 'master plan' for future expansion, a draft version of which was initially drawn up by Friedrich Ludwig von Sckell. Maxvorstadt was the first major planned project outside the former city walls: on Ludwigstraße, Friedrich von Gärtner was responsible for the Bavarian State Library, Ludwigskirche (Ludwig's Church) and the university, which Ludwig ordered transferred from Landshut to Munich in 1826. Gärtner was also responsible for the Feldherrnhalle and Siegestor (which bookend Ludwigstraße) as well as Briennerstraße, which passes his Wittelsbacher Platz and the obelisk at Karolinenplatz, erected in commeroration of the 30,000 Bavarians killed during Napoleon's Russian campaign.

While Munich artists, architects and builders benefited greatly from the building boom and the king's efforts at creating a neo-classical capital, the population soon grew weary of his anachronistic ideas of kingship. Initially, Ludwig had appeared to be a progressive ruler, but his deep-seated reactionary philosophy came increasingly to the fore, particularly after social unrest in France sparked off the French July Revolution of 1830. Up until 1848, this manifested itself primarily in constant disputes with the Bavarian government and the Munich city council, which, in short, objected to his far too autocratic predilections, often revolving around his opposition to political liberalism and to Protestantism. Ludwig's inability to accept the changing nature between monarch and subject would cost him dearly.

In 1800, Munich had a population of around 36,000. By 1830, five years into Ludwig's reign, this had more than doubled to 77,000, rising again to 95,000 by 1840. In the same year, the population of Bavaria had reached 4.37 million, most of whom lived in rural areas and worked on the land rather than in cities, reflecting that Munich was still the capital of an overwhelmingly agricultural state. On a wider level, the German Confederation, created in the wake of Napoleon's defeat, was still far from a unified state in the British and French sense, and its industrial and political development was, with a few regional exceptions, much more patchy. In essence, Germany was still a patchwork (admittedly, with far fewer patches) of large, medium and small sovereign states, which manifested extremely uneven political, social and cultural developments.

Moreover, socio-economic problems were mounting across post-Napoleonic Europe, often associated with backward-looking rulers clashing with proponents of a more modern or 'liberal' concept of the role society should play in moulding states structures. In France, popular disaffection reached its peak with the February Revolution of 1848, which toppled King Louis-Philippe,and proved to be the catalyst for a number of revolutions across the German Confederation. The aims of the revolutionaries were multifarious, ranging from liberal political demands for constitutional rule and German national unification to demands for improvements in working conditions and greater press freedoms. While, to a larger or smaller degree, similar demands existed in Munich, Ludwig I ultimately – and rather comically – lost his throne primarily because of his refusal to give up his mistress, Lola Montez (1820-1861).

Lola Montez & Revolution

Shortly before taking the Bavarian throne, Ludwig I had a 'beauty gallery' erected in the Residenz, for which he commissioned court painter Joseph Stieler to paint Munich's most beautiful ladies. Over the course of around 30 years, 36 oil paintings were completed. One of the last portraits painted was that of Lola Montez, which carried the inscription: 'Countess Maria of Landsfeld, born in Seville 1823'. While the reference to 'countess' was just about correct, her birthplace as Spain most definitely was not.

Born in Ireland to an English army officer as Elizabeth Rosanna Gilbert, she ran away at 19 to marry a Lieutenant Thomas James. When, five years later, the marriage had fallen apart, she started a career as a dancer in London, before setting off to tour European cities, typically passing herself off as Lola Montez, a Spanish dancer. Turning up in Munich in 1846 for a show, she somehow manoeuvred for herself an audience with the king, who was quickly smitten, prompting the 60-year-old monarch to write to a friend: "My life has got a new impetus and I am once again young.'

Though perhaps not his lover, Montez soon became Ludwig's closest confidant and advisor, much to the chagrin of his ministers, the Bavarian aristocracy, the Catholic Church and in the end most of the Munich population. Montez revelled in the attention and she ostentatiously paraded her exalted position and influence around the royal court and in political circles, ignoring any public scandal her actions were seen to provoke. The king showered her with gifts and her annual allowance of 10,000 florins was around 4,000 more than cabinet ministers received. Against the will of his ministers, on 25 August 1847 Ludwig handed Lola the grandiose title of Countess of Landsfeld. From then on periodic outbreaks of violence descended on the city until matters came to a head in January and February 1848. When Montez took a walk on 9 February along Ludwigstraße and Theatinerstraße she was roughed up and had to flee to the safety of the Theatinerkirche, before receiving a military escort to the Residenz. The king was enraged, and his response was to close the university until the winter semester and to order all non-Munich students to leave the city. This succeeded only in redirecting the public's anger towards Montez's palace on Barer Straße, which was plundered and wrecked.

The closure of the university disrupted the city's economy and provided an increasing number of citizens with a definitive anti-Ludwig banner to rally around. Ludwig subsequently offered to reopen the university, though, reflecting his inability to fully comprehend the precariousness of his position, not until the summer. That the city was prepared to resort to rioting and in the process to devastate a number of pubs and breweries because of the seemingly trivial raising of the price of beer, as had happened in May 1844, should have provided Ludwig with an insight into the mood of his subjects when antagonised. The furious population rejected the king's offer and demanded the expulsion of Lola Montez and the immediate reopening of the university. The fall of the French king on 24 February and the subsequent huge unrest around the German Confederation poured oil onto an already fiery atmosphere in Munich.

Further rioting followed, including the plundering of the city arsenal on St.-Jakobs-Platz. Spending money on the military had never been a priority for the art-loving Ludwig, and in a time of crisis he very much doubted that he could rely on its support. Popular demands for the abolition of oppressive press censorship, reform of legal proceedings, added to demands for new elections and police reforms – all granted – proved too much for Ludwig's anachronistic ideas of monarchy. Ultimately, he could not accept handing over what he thought were issues for him to decide upon alone, and when protests resurfaced in March with the rumour that Lola Montez had returned to the city, he meekly abdicated.

It appears ludicrous that the king of Germany's third largest state could be overthrown because of his obsession with a dancer while at the same

Anglo-Irish Elizabeth Rosanna Gilbert, or 'Lola Montez', was key to the fall of King Ludwig I

time much of the German Confederation was up in arms demanding profound political and social reforms. Unrest relating to lack of reform had been brewing in many parts of Bavaria for some years prior to 1848. These socio-economic and political issues certainly prepared the ground for what was to come. But Ludwig's fall was the direct consequence of his patent inability to come to terms with his obsession with Lola Montez, itself intrinsically linked to his vision of himself as an autocratic ruler: as he saw it, if he preferred to take advice from a dancer rather than his ministers, it was his business, and his alone.

On 19 March he released his abdication proclamation: 'I am laying down my crown in favour of my loving son, the crown prince, Maximilian. I ruled true to the constitution.' Munich had lost its greatest art patron, and when Anna Mary Howitt passed him in the street in 1850, he was still struggling to come to terms with his deposition. He never did.

For the rest of the German Confederation, though some concessions had been won by the end of 1848, it was clear that reformers and revolutionaries had failed in their aim of creating a unified country. Though far from a radical, Bavaria's King Maximilian II (1811-1864) ruled in a more collegiate manner than his father, seeking advice from sometimes innumerable experts before making decisions. Moreover, he was considerably more open to reform than his father and made important political concessions (the simplification of the voting system to Bavaria's second chamber, for example), while he also relaxed press freedoms and implemented much-needed reforms to the justice system. He was also responsible for a handful of significant building projects, including the majestic neo-gothic Maximilanstraße, nowadays home to some of Europe's most exclusive and most expensive fashion stores, and the Maximilianeum, today the seat of the Bavarian parliament, but originally conceived as a centre of excellence for students. Moreover, Maximilian was fascinated by science and literature. He promoted Munich as a centre of scientific research and echoing his father's transfer of the university from Landshut to Munich, he founded the Technische Universität München (TUM), so important in Munich's contemporary identity as a high-tech city of research and development. Indeed, his 'Symposien' meetings regularly attracted a gathering of Germany's literati and best scientific brains, including, for example, Berlin-born writer Paul Heyse (1830-1914), chemist Justus Freiherr von Liebig (1830-1873) and historian Wilhelm von Doenniges (1814-1872).

Munich was modernising quickly, and it was under the reign of Maximilian II that monarchical control over the city recognisably receded. Munich's population grew exponentially during the next 50 years. In 1852 the city had around

95,000 inhabitants, rising over the next two years by more than 21,000 with the incorporation of the Au, Haidhausen and Giesing areas on the right bank of the Isar, and in the process almost doubling the geographical size of the city. With this, particularly in the case of Au, Munich acquired a large number of very poor, who, as in all Europe's cities, were never far from destitution and could afford only the most basic living conditions. Further incorporations, such as Ramersdorf (1864), Untersendling (1877) Neuhausen and Schwabing (1890), and Bogenhausen (1892), once again hugely increased the size of the city and lifted its population by 1900 to 499,932.

The city was hit by cholera epidemics in 1854 and 1873-1874, a disease that shaped the later part of the career of the great Munich scientist Max von Pettenkofer (1818-1901). In a bid to reduce the effects of cholera in the city, Pettenkofer successfully implemented numerous hygiene measures such as a modern drainage system and a clean water supply. Similarly, expanding industrialisation drove further modernisation of the city's infrastructure: Munich's first central train station opened in 1839 and better transportation within the city was provided with the establishment of a horse-drawn tram in October 1876, partially electrified in 1895, fully by 1900, while the city had already received its first gaslights by 1850. The city was now being planned and constructed largely independently of the Residenz, best symbolised by the fact that it was the wealth of Carl von Eichtal that paid for the building of the Gärtnerplatz quarter of the city, with its fabulous properties available to buy and rent.

Munich held little attraction for Ludwig II, Maximilian's successor in 1864, who nevertheless turned out to be Bavaria's most famous monarch by far, primarily on account of his apparent 'madness' and his propensity for building monumental castles in beautiful Alpine locations across Bavaria.

With Ludwig's attention not focused on the capital, Munich gained further independence from old-style meddling monarchs, spectacularly evident in Ludwig's relationship with the composer Richard Wagner (1813-1883). The city's National Theatre premiered Wagner's *Tristan and Isolde* in June 1865, later *Die Meistersinger von Nürnberg*, *Das Rheingold* and *Die Walküre*. But Ludwig was particularly aggrieved when his plan for a prohibitively expensive theatre for 1,500 to 1,700 people on the banks of the Isar met huge resistance across the city and was consequently cancelled. It is quite possible that his castles dotted around the Bavarian Alps and his patronage of Wagner would have guaranteed Ludwig II lasting fame. However, his death in Lake Starnberg in 1886 under mysterious circumstances, shortly after his arrest on the grounds of his 'madness', has ensured that his name carries significance that, in reality, his achievements hardly merit.

By 1910, the Wittelsbach royal family may have had the eighth costliest civil list in the world, but the reality was that Munich – and wider Bavaria – had long ceased to depend on a monarch for its principal direction. Prince Regent Luitpold (1821-1912) was primarily interested in upholding what he saw as the dignity of the monarchy, and ceremonial events were central to how he saw the role of the Bavarian royal family. The 'Prinzregentenzeit' (Prince Regent Era, 1886-1912) is now seen as Munich's golden years, though this has more to do with art than any wider political influence the city had. While political power did indeed now lay increasingly in the hands of politicians, many of the orders no longer emanated from the Bavarian capital. Power had shifted to Berlin, the capital of Prussia, very much Munich's *bête noire*. Otto von Bismarck's (1815-1898) Prussian-led German unification – constituting a 'small Germany' (meaning without Austria) – was born out of three successive wars: against Denmark over Schleswig-Holstein in 1864; against Austria, Bavaria, Saxony, Hanover, Württemberg and Baden in 1866; and against France in 1870, which resulted in the founding of the German Empire in 1871 at Versailles.

The new Germany has been aptly described by Matthew Jefferies, as an 'idiosyncratic mix of absolute monarchy, parliamentary representation and plebiscitary democracy'. A total of 25 state governments were represented in the Bundesrat (Federal Council) while the Reichstag (the German national parliament) was elected on universal male suffrage, decades in advance of most countries. This was a federal empire, and the German states retained their monarchs and a degree of autonomy, few more so than Bavaria, particularly relating to internal matters, such as education, the arts and religion. But no matter how it was wrapped up, no matter the concessions, Bavaria was now part of a country led by Bismarck's Prussia.

The building of the Neues Rathaus on Marienplatz entailed the destruction of many historic buildings. Above is a photo of the first section of the new building

Bohemian Munich

> Munich was resplendent … Young artists with small round hats perched on the backs of their heads, loosely tied cravats and no walking sticks – carefree young men who pay their rent with an occasional sketch – are out walking, seeking moods of inspiration in the bright blue morning sky and letting their eyes stray after the girls.

Gladius Dei, from which the above quote is taken, was, of course, an ironic 1902 short story by Thomas Mann (1875-1955) set in Munich and loosely concerned with the city's perceived role in the world of art, architecture and wider German culture. While Mann, who lived in the city between 1894 and 1933, was happy to gently mock his adopted home, it was true, nevertheless,

Finished in 1854, Munich's Glaspalast owed its inspiration to London's Crystal Palace, home to Britain's Great Exhibition of 1851. It was one of Europe's finest exhibition centres

that *fin de siècle* Munich had developed into one of the Europe's most important artistic and literary centres. After all, many of Mann's greatest works were conceived and written in the city.

Bismarck's unification had initially given a huge boost to a Germany already rapidly developing into the world's most dynamic economy. Modernisation, however, brought with it new dislocations and challenges, typically related to a growing proletariat and a massive influx of workers to the towns and cities from the countryside. The 1871 Munich census reveals that the city's population stood at 169,000, and leapt to 285,000 by 1888, raising the perennial problem of insufficient housing. Munich's skyline was also changing, often with little regard for possible historic significance of exisiting structures, most particularly in the case of the decision to pull down the city's medieval inner wall. Similarly, as the Altes Rathaus was hemmed in, unable to be enlarged suf-

ficiently, the Neues Rathaus was built in stages between 1867 and its completion in 1904. Located on Marienplatz, this construction entailed pulling down a number of historic buildings dating from the 15th and 16th centuries.
As industrialisation intensified, Munich became a centre of locomotive building as well as of the production of precision instruments, while it also started to become a substantial exporter of beer. Firms such as Pschorr, Hofbräukeller, Augustinerkeller, Löwenbrauerei and Spatenbräu benefited from Carl von Linde's (1842-1934) revolutionary cooling machines. In addition, the improvement in water quality due to the pioneering work of Max von Pettenkofer enabled a handful of Munich-based breweries to grow into successful medium-sized concerns and to dominate the market in the city and in its hinterland. In 1853 the Schrannenhalle, on the edge ofViktualienmarkt, became Munich's first glass and iron construction, followed in 1854 by the huge Glaspalast (for the German Exhibition, in the manner of London's Great Exhibition of 1851), which quickly became the venue for Munich's world-renowned art exhibitions. In fact, as as will be seen in chapter 6, Munich was as important an art location as any other city in Europe at this time. Munich's 1869 exhibition drew in tens of thousands of visitors, and by Ludwig II's death in 1886, the city boasted 796 painters and 148 sculptors. Furthermore, Munich was the first Germany city to put on an exhibition of electricity, with thousands turning up to see the spectacular Glaspalast lit up, while electricity became available to the city from a central generating point in 1891.
Although a relatively liberal reform of voting rights had taken place in 1869, until 1893 there was the situation that even though adult men aged over 25 in Munich could vote for their national representatives in the Reichstag in Berlin, severely restrictive property ownership qualification criteria meant that many were ineligible to vote in Munich's local elections.
Peter Claus Hartmann estimates that in the closing decades of the 19th century 53 to 55 per cent of the Munich population was from the newly emerged working-class milieu, of which a significant minority were periodically unemployed, poor, undernourished and desperately in need of decent housing. Commensurate to the rise of the German working class was the rise of German social democracy, though the two were far from synonymous. The Social Democratic Party (SPD) first won representation to the city council in 1893, but it did not achieve real influence until further voting reforms in 1908. By

1912, the SPD was the biggest party in the German Reichstag; on the eve of the First World War, in 1914, the party represented the largest faction in the Munich Rathaus. Contemporaneously, Munich's population had continued its inexorable growth, due largely to another spate of incorporations: Nymphenburg in 1899, Thalkirchen and Laim in 1900, Forstenried in 1912 and Milbertshofen, Berg am Laim, Moosach and, finally, Oberföhring in 1913, the last being significant because it included Föhring, which had played such a significant role in Munich's foundation by Heinrich XII in the 12th century. By 1900, the incorporations and the influx of people from the countryside meant around half of Munich's almost 500,000 residents had not been born in the city.

During the Prinzregentenzeit tourists began to flock to the Bavarian capital in large numbers, attracted by the city's baroque architecture, its numerous superb churches and impressive grand boulevards, and to take in the atmosphere of such a vital centre of art, not forgetting it was a royal capital. Although the Munich Secession of 1892 had signalled that all was not completely rosy within Munich's revered art community, the city was still a star attraction for foreign artists, and a new generation of painters emerged, most notably The Blue Rider (Der Blaue Reiter), formed by pioneers of abstract art such as Wassily Kandinsky (1866-1944), Franz Marc (1880-1916), Gabriele Münter (1877-1962), August Macke (1887-1914) and Paul Klee (1879-1940). The centre of bohemian Munich life was Schwabing, which drew writers attracted to a blossoming literary scene. And in addition to Thomas Mann, writers and poets of the calibre of Mann's brother, Heinrich (1871-1950), Rainer Maria Rilke (1875-1926), Stefan George (1868-1933), Ludwig Thoma (1867-1921) and Frank Wedekind (1864-1918) lived in the city. The magazine *Jugend* complemented the nature-inspired *Jugendstil* that elegantly furnished the interiors and façades of a number of Munich buildings, while *Simplicissimus* magazine, often lit up by Thomas Theodor Heine's (1867-1948) ingenious illustrations, provided cutting satirical comment on social and political life in Imperial Germany.

There was, however, another side to the art metropolis image. The Thomas Mann extract above is from a story about a confrontation between an art dealer and a man of extreme piety, who sees little more than smut and vulgarity in modern art. In short, Mann was highlighting that there was far from universal agreement that the development of modernism, particularly in art, was entirely desirable. Moreover, the image often portrayed of artistic Munich and bohemian Schwabing as the *real* Munich – a Munich destroyed by the First World War – is at best disingenuous. On the eve of the war, the city had become a teeming metropolis of hundreds of thousands of people, a magnet to tourists and a thriving economic centre, if never quite an industrial one. On the one hand, this was a city of neo-classical architecture, opera, superb museums and respected theatre. It was a home of German *Kultur*, a word that imparts a sense of 'high culture' and entails intellectual and artistic discourse in a manner not quite suggested in the English word 'culture'. Similarly, it was a city of the almost mythical German *Bürgertum*, the educated and respectable professional (in reality, a tiny minority) of Thomas Mann's *Buddenbrooks*. On the other hand, there was another Munich: a reactionary city with heightened intolerance and a marked antisemitism, a city with a largely sidelined working class: poorly paid factory workers, the unemployed and the destitute living in slums.

Whichever image is more accurate – city of art, city of reaction, or both – 1914 to 1918 engendered a seismic shift. Of course, continuities and changes define epochs, but four years of devastating war plus a short-lived left-wing

Enthusiastic Bavarian troops set off in 1914 from Munich for war. The message reads: 'From Munich via Metz to Paris'

revolution succeeded in radicalising Munich to such a degree that by 1920 the city had become an infamous haven for Germany's most radical right-wing agitators. This radically altered the face and reputation of Munich forever, and ultimately led to a catastrophe of unprecedented proportions.

1918 & Revolution

Between the 1940s and the 1970s, a number of historians spent far too long searching for a 'fault line' in the 'German character' that would help identify the causes of the so-called 'German problem' (R D O'Butler and most popularly William Shirer, to name but two). Little of this work added much to the understanding of the catastrophic first half of the 20th century and relied a great deal on a teleological reading of history. Ian Kershaw, in his biography of Adolf Hitler (1889-1945), is rather more perceptive:

> The First World War made Hitler possible. Without ... the trauma of war, defeat and revolution, without the political radicalisation of German society that this trauma brought about, the demagogue would have been without an audience for his raucous, hate-filled message ... Without the war, a Hitler on the Chancellor's seat that had been occupied by Bismarck would have been unthinkable.

While the declaration of war in 1914 may not have resulted in the overwhelming jubilation of the popular imagination (on 28/29 July, shortly before war was declared, there were an estimated 500,000 anti-war demonstrators on Germany's streets), there is no doubt that huge numbers of people across Europe welcomed the war. Since the fall of Bismarck in 1890 much of the German population had bought into the prevailing idea of Germany becoming an influential world power in line with its rapidly growing economic might. While all the great European powers were to varying degrees complicit in ensuring war broke out, it would be accurate to describe Germany's role as the principal provocateur. The crowds of pro-war supporters celebrating the declaration of war on 2 August 1914, such as that at Munich's Odeonsplatz, which included the 25-year-old Austrian Adolf Hitler (1889-1945), got neither the war they expected nor the war they wanted.

Kasier Wilhelm II's (1859-1941) declaration in August 1914 that 'I no longer recognise parties; I recognise only Germans,' was at best a desperate hope that Germany's major social, political and class cleavages could be overcome by war. Initial military success against Russia lifted German hopes of a quick victory but by Christmas 1914 a procession of trenches from Switzerland to the English Channel had set the scene for the impasse and the carnage that would come to characterise the horror of the Western Front.

In Munich, shortages of basic foodstuff, clothes and coal were all too apparent by 1915, and 1916 saw hundreds of people (predominantly women and children) angrily protesting outside the Rathaus for an increase in the bread ration. The harsh winter of 1916/17 was a further low point for the population, magnified when it was soon caught up in the Europe-wide flu pandemic. By mid-1918, Munich had lost 13,725 soldiers to the war, the tide of which had turned decisively against Germany. Munich's population increasingly identified the enfolding catastrophe with the hated 'Preußen', Prussians. Rumours of cutting hop quotas (for the production of beer) while Prussian schnapps makers were well-provided for aroused Bavarian ire, with the left-wing Munich writer Ernst Toller typically later complaining: 'Just because the Prussian swine don't mind bad beer, Bavarians also had to swallow dishwater.' In addition, a huge swell of animosity was growing against the city's own royal house, namely the Wittelsbachs, now led by King Ludwig III, Prince Leopold and Crown Prince Rupprecht, who were all implicated to varying degrees in Germany's increasingly dictatorial military leadership of Paul von Hindenburg (1847-1934) and Erich Ludendorff (1865-1937). War-weary, hungry and angry, the population resorted to strikes and protests as a way of forcing change. By late 1918, France and Britain – since 1917 supplemented by the United States and its huge resources – were overwhelming the German military effort, prompting Ludendorff and Hindenburg to abdicate responsibility by choosing to hand over accepting the catastrophic military defeat to civilian authorities. The military had in effect washed its hands of a war it had so desired, it had led in an ever-dictatorial manner and, even in the weeks leading up to what was by then inevitable defeat, it had promised it would win. The reality was that during the First World War, Germany had lost 1.6 million men with a further 4 million wounded. Defeat came as an earth-shattering shock; revolution in its aftermath was not.

The 1917 October Russian Revolution (led by Lenin, who had lived for a short time in the Schwabing quarter of Munich) provided inspiration for left-wing revolutionaries across Europe. On 5 November 1918 sailors at Kiel in northern Germany disobeyed orders to go on what was seen as a suicide mission against the British fleet, and soon afterwards rumours flew across Germany that Kiel was in the hands of revolutionaries. The revolution in Bavaria preceded that across the Reich, was more radical than that in Berlin and left a searing impression on the population's psyche, nowhere more so than in Munich. Moreover, it profoundly affected Adolf Hitler, who witnessed much of the most radical phase unfold.

The Bavarian revolution started at Theresienwiese, location of Munich's annual Oktoberfest celebrations (not as incongruous as it might sound: it is a large open space and a favourite location for huge meetings). On 7 November, crowds gathered to hear anti-war speeches by among others Kurt Eisner (1867-1919), the local leader of the USPD (Independent Social Democratic Party of Germany, reflecting a split in German social democracy), who riled right-wing Bavarians not only because of his Prussian background, but also because he was Jewish. But the revolution in Munich was about much more than Münchners, as David Clay Large has noted on the make-up of the crowds at Theresienwiese

> [M]any radical Saxon loyalists from the local Krupp works; mutinous soldiers and sailors who had abandoned their units; rebellious farmers brought in by their leaders, the blind demagogue Ludwig Gandorfer; a smattering of Schwabing bohemians; thousands of women and teenagers; and the usual assortment of beer-hall rowdies ready to follow any fast talker who promised a little excitement.

The gatherings, however, seemed to reveal little appetite for, as one eye witness later recorded, 'continued war nor revolutionary tribunals and burning stately homes.' Instead, at this time, for many the main priority was an immediate end to the war.

The crowd 'marched hemmed in by the impatient throng', recorded novelist Oskar Maria Graf (1894-1967), and headed towards the barracks complex in the north of the city. Badly under-estimating the seriousness of the fast-

Crowds at Maximiliansbrücke greet Freikorps troops heading towards central Munich in 1919

changing situation throughout Germany, the Bavarian king, Ludwig III, was at this time idling around the English Garden, seemingly impervious to the events taking shape a few minutes' walk away. Legend has it that a passer-by spotted the king and advised him in deep Bavarian, 'Majestät! Genga S'hoam, sonnst passiert Eahna wos!', roughly translated as: 'Majesty! Go home, or something's going to happen to you!' At 7 o'clock in the evening, with the support of the soldiers, major public buildings were occupied and within an hour or so the Wittelsbach royal family had wisely fled Munich. Eisner led his followers into the Bavarian parliament and proclaimed Bavaria a republic. The House of Wittelsbach, rulers of Bavaria for more than seven centuries, was only the first German monarchy to be toppled. On 9 November it was followed by the abdication of Emperor Wilhelm II in Berlin, the German Empire was history and by 1919 it had been replaced with the Weimar Republic, Germany's first democracy, named after the city in which its constitution was hammered out.

While peace officially came to Europe on 11 November 1918, Munich was about to be engulfed in a period of utter turmoil that would have far-reaching and long-term consequences. In the elections to the Bavarian parliament in

January 1919, Eisner and his USPD were all but wiped out in the polls, winning around 2.5 per cent of the vote. But that was not enough for some. On 21 February, when on his way to resign as leader of the provisional government, Eisner was murdered by a right-wing student, Graf Anton von Arco-Valley (1897-1945). The assassination sparked a period of chaos and violence on the city's streets, culminating in April, when radical revolutionaries attempted to erect the so-called Räterepublik in Munich in the hope of imposing a Leninist-style regime across Bavaria.

Freikorps units (radical right-wing, nationalist troops) together with troops from Prussia and Württemberg headed for Munich and quickly defeated the revolutionaries. Atrocities were committed on both sides, with reprisals begetting reprisals, which claimed more than (an estimated) 600 lives before Munich's 'liberation'. Munich's reputation, garnered through the centuries, as a city of art, a city that attempted to define itself as throbbing with an almost mythical *Gemütlichkeit* (an over-used and very elastic word, perhaps best summed up as 'sociability') was quickly losing its sheen.

It would be difficult to exaggerate the impact on the city's political consciousness of the events in Munich between November 1918 and May 1919, particularly the Räterepublik, described – particularly by many middle-class Münchners – as a *Schreckensherrschaft*, a 'reign of terror'. With the help of right-wing propaganda, the period implanted in middle-class Munich the notion that Bolshevik and Jewish forces had attempted to take over the state, the result being, as described by Richard F Hamilton, that 'much of the city's middle-class population lived with a continuous siege mentality.' But just as important was that the huge level of violence meted out by right-wing troops was painted as a legitimate restoration of order and discipline. Image had conquered reality, the consequence of which was that the stage was set for Munich to become a bastion of right-wing extremism.

Capital of the Movement

After failing his entrance exams to Vienna's Academy of Fine Arts in September 1907, the prospects for the homeless 18-year-old Adolf Hitler reached rock-bottom in the winter of 1909/10 as he joined the other unfortunates searching for a bed in one of the city's doss-houses. It was in Vienna that Hitler imbibed various racist, right-wing tracts and listened to radical speeches that helped his still nascent *Weltanschauung*, or 'world view'. He arrived in Munich – possibly motivated by his eagerness to evade the Austrian draft – on a sunny 25 May 1913 and was soon earning a modest living painting city scenes, mainly from postcards sold in bars and cafes. With the declaration of war in 1914, he enthusiastically joined the Bavarian army (as an Austrian, something he was not legally entitled to do) and it seemed his life had finally found some meaning. Germany's defeat in 1918, therefore, was a personal catastrophe for Hitler.

On 12 September 1919, for his role in the German army reporting on radical organisations in Munich, Hitler attended a meeting of the German Workers' Party (Deutsche Arbeiterpartei, DAP) in the Sterneckerbräu. In short, having impressed DAP leaders by interrupting and castigating one of the speakers, he joined the party and soon became its leader. Renamed the National Socialist German Workers' Party (Nationalsozialistische Deutsche Arbeiterpartei, NSDAP), its 'immutable' party programme of 25 points was announced on 4 February 1920 to a mass of supporters at the Hofbräuhaus in central Munich. Hitler quickly became one of the leading far-right radicals in the city, particularly noted for his at times 'mesmerising' speeches, typically focusing on the 'November criminals' (responsible, in his view, for Germany losing the war and for signing the Versailles peace treaty), socialism and the baleful influence – as he saw it – of 'Jewish international finance capital'. He regularly attracted many thousands of supporters to his speeches in Munich beer halls, while anywhere between 2,000 and 8,000 would gather at the city's largest venue, the Zirkus-Krone-Bau (today the Circus Krone), to hear him speak. By the end of 1920, it is thought the NSDAP had in the region of 2,000 members, which increased to some 55,000 members during the period of hyper-inflation in mid-1923, a period characterised by heightened anti-Weimar Republic sentiment across Bavaria and the rest of Germany.

The elections to the German National Assembly of January 1919 (to draw up the country's future democracy) came in the wake of the December 1918 Spartacist uprising in Berlin, crushed by the army and right-wing Freikorps troops, and were followed by further unrest in the capital and many other places around the country. The prospects for German democracy looked bleak. The election, however, resulted in a national coalition of the Social ic Party (38 per cent), the Catholic Centre (Zentrum, 19.7 per cent) ...eral German Democratic Party (DDP, 18.5 per cent), all committed democratic parties.

It is important to note the different levels of German elections – local, state and national – and the sometimes dissimilar results they threw up. In contrast to the disaster for Kurt Eisner's USPD at the Bavarian state elections of January 1919, in the Munich local mayoral elections of early 1919, the party's 32 per cent was the highest of all parties, followed by the conservative Bavarian People's Party (BVP) with 28 per cent and the Majority Social Democratic Party (MSPD) with 18 per cent. In spite of the result, the left's compromise candidate, Eduard Schmid (1861-1933), of the MSPD, became Munich's very first democratic mayor, serving until replaced by Karl Scharnagl (1881-1963) of the Bavarian People's Party in 1925, who served until the Nazi takeover of Germany in 1933 and again between 1945 and 1948.

The elections to the German national parliament, the Reichstag, of 6 June 1920 proved to be a disaster for Germany's National Assembly coalition parties as all three suffered heavy losses. In the end, the first of a series of weak coalitions was cobbled together, which soon had rampant inflation to deal with, fuelled in part by a policy of 'fulfilment', whereby the national government attempted to highlight its inability to pay its reparations to the Allies as part of the Treaty of Versailles. The sheer scale of the hyperinflation by 1923 can be gauged from a few figures relating to the Munich economy: in 1918 an egg had cost 25 pfennigs, rising to 5,000 German marks in the summer of 1923 and 80 million marks by November. Similarly, a pound of butter rose from 2 marks in 1918 to 150,000 marks in the summer of 1923, surging to the astronomical figure of 6 billion marks by November 1923.

This policy of fulfilment enraged people on all sides of the political spectrum, but it was most telling with nationalists and the far right, particularly those in conservative Bavaria. By late 1923, relations between the right-wing Bavarian government in Munich, led by Bavarian Minister President Gustav Ritter von Kahr (1862-1934), and the leaders of the more liberal national government in Berlin had reached crisis point. When in November the Bavarian authorities dithered about whether to attempt a 'March on Berlin' (a *coup d'état* inspired by Mussolini's October 1922 so-called 'March on Rome'), Hitler took the initiative. He planned – in the loosest meaning of the word – to lead a right-wing Bavarian putsch against German democracy. First, however, he needed to convince Munich.

Hoping to force the Bavarian government's hand, at 8.30pm on 8 November Hitler and a band of his brownshirted SA (*Sturmabteilung*, the Nazis' paramilitary wing) stormed a meeting at Munich's Bürgerbräukeller – just as Bavarian Minister President Kahr was delivering a speech to a crowd of around 3,000 people – and declared that the national revolution had broken out. In truth, nothing of the sort had happened. Promising he was in step with Hitler's plans, Kahr was released, at which point he proceeded to inform the Bavarian authorities he wanted nothing to do with the putsch attempt. Realising the hopelessness of the situation, Hitler decided on a demonstration through the city in the vain hope of stirring Münchners into an uprising. At midday on 9 November, around 2,000 mostly armed men marched from the Bürgerbräukeller, over Ludwigsbrücke towards Tal and on to Marienplatz. Turning right down Residenzstraße, former home of the Wittelsbach royal family, hoping to get to the War Ministry, they were stopped at Odeonsplatz by a police cordon. The firing of a gun sparked a hail of bullets from both sides, leaving 14 putschists and four policemen dead. Hitler's ill-thought-out attempt to takeover Germany from his base in Munich had floundered before it had got going.

In the wake of the failed 'Beer Hall Putsch' the Nazi Party was proscribed and its leaders jailed, albeit with lenient sentences. Hitler, for attempting to take over the state, received a five-year sentence, which he carried out in a furnished room in the prison at nearby Landsberg. He was released on 20 December 1924, having served less than eight months.

By the time of his release, Hitler's world view was fully crystallised. To be clear, National Socialist ideology was neither unique nor new. While a straight line should not be drawn from the mid-1800s to 1933, the roots of Nazi ideology can be traced to theories derived in the 19th century. Its three main tenets were, in short, pseudo-scientific notions encompassing crude racial-anthropology; theories of racial-hygiene or 'eugenics'; and racial antisemitism. This world view paradoxically saw a relationship between Marxism and international finance capital, culminating in Russian Bolshevism, which, according to Hitler's *Mein Kampf*, was 'the attempt undertaken by the Jews in the 20th century to achieve world domination'. Hitler's world view, therefore, saw history as a (pseudo-Darwinistic) racial struggle combined with a rabid

Hitler and Goebbels attend an architecture exhibition at the 'Haus der Deutschen Kunst' on 22 January 1938. Looking on between Hitler and Goebbels, in glasses, slightly behind, is the Nazi mayor of Munich, Karl Fiehler

antisemitism and a belief that Germany's future could be secured only through the conquering of *Lebensraum* (living space) at the expense of Russia. These basic beliefs never altered.

By 1925, the Nazi message was struggling to locate a following on any sizeable scale, largely because the Weimar Republic was experiencing a period between 1924 and 1929 of 'relative stabilisation'. The Wall Street Crash of 1929, however, with its devastating effect of generating mass unemployment, changed everything. In December 1924, the NSDAP had won just 5.9 per cent in the Munich local city elections; in 1929 it won 15.4 per cent. In the national Reichstag elections of 1928 and 1930, the party's share rose from 10.7 per cent to 21.8 per cent in Munich (jumping from 2.6 per cent to 18.3 per cent across Germany), reaching a high point in the July 1932 election of 28.9 per cent across the city (37.3 per cent in Germany). Though fewer votes than across Germany as an average, by this time, a significant minority of the Munich population had clearly decided that in such catastrophic times the Nazis could be the answer. Voters across Germany had been abandoning the centre ground for some time, and by the Reichstag elections on 6 November

After the Nazi takeover of 1933, the area around Königsplatz became the 'heartlands' of the Nazi Party

1932, the most popular parties in Germany were the communist KPD and the NDSAP (both openly anti-democratic), the members of which in many areas of Germany were involved in little short of street warfare.

The electoral stalemate of autumn 1932, with no possibility of working coalitions, provides the background to Hitler eventually being handed the chancellorship in January 1933, even though the Nazi vote had dropped by 2 million in the November 1932 election.

In Munich, the BVP mayor, Karl Scharnagl, was forced out of office and replaced by Karl Fiehler (1895-1969), a long-time Nazi Party member and participant in Hitler's 1923 failed putsch. The nature of National Socialist rule soon became apparent. With all other political parties banned and no opposition tolerated, the Nazis began to build a brutal dictatorship. Dachau, just 20 km north-west of Munich and already open by 22 March 1933, became the model for hundreds of future concentration camps. From its earliest days, it was where the Nazis imprisoned in inhumane conditions scores of communists, social democrats, homosexuals, Jews and other so-called 'undesirables'.

Similarly, Munich was to be the model National Socialist city. In 1935, Hitler made Munich's informal position as 'Capital of the Movement' (i.e. of the Nazi Party) official, providing the city with a new coat of arms, including the all-important Nazi swastika. Moreover, the Nazis set to work on altering the Munich cityscape, most famously the areas around Königsplatz and Karolinenplatz, including architect Paul Ludwig Troost's (1878-1934) Honour Temples (which still stand in a reduced form, without pillars) commemorating the Nazi dead in the failed 1923 putsch. Others still extant include the imposing Haus der Deutschen Kunst (now Haus der Kunst) and the former air force building, now used by the Bavarian finance ministry. The majority of Hitler's building plans for the city, however, were never realised. The 14-metre-long model of Hitler's 'Great Axis' (*Große Achse*), detailing megalomaniacal plans for Munich, the focal point being a 200-metre-high memorial to Nazism, now appear as little more than monumental caricatures of Klenze's and Gärtner's neo-classical 19th-century creations.

The building of Haus der Deutschen Kunst and the title of 'Capital of German Art' were part of the regime's plan to place Munich once again at the centre of the German art world. In contrast to turn-of-the-century Munich, however, this centre of art was not to be left to the likes of bohemians from Schwabing; it was deemed much too important for that. In order to educate the city in the virtues of 'true' art, it was deemed that the city's population would have to compare the Nazi-approved works in the Haus der Deutschen Kunst with an exhibition entitled 'Degenerate Art', typically featuring deliberately badly hung modern pieces by, for example, one-time Munich artists Franz Marc, Wassily Kandinsky and Paul Klee, as well as Pablo Picasso and Henri Matisse. Both exhibitions opened in 1937, though, much to the disgust of its promoters, the so-called Degenerate Art exhibition attracted much larger numbers (over two million visitors), as it did when subsequently on tour around Germany,

Munich's link with the Nazis was brought more into focus to the wider world when on 29 September 1938 British Prime Minister Neville Chamberlain agreed at the Munich Conference to the handing over of the Sudetenland to Germany in a futile bid to prevent another European conflagration. War was temporarily averted, and in the process the name of Munich became inextricably linked with the infamous British and French policy of 'appeasement'.

Hitler speaking at the Bürgerbräukeller at the annual commemoration of the 1923 Nazi putsch attempt. Moments after Hitler left on 8 November 1939, a bomb exploded in the pillar behind

A year later, on 1 September 1939, German troops invaded Poland and Europe was once again at war. By the time Munich surrendered to US troops in April 1945, the city lay in ruins, its population destitute and shamed by its complicity in the Holocaust. As with other towns and cities across Germany, at the height of Nazi foreign policy triumphs, between 1938 and 1941, Hitler's popularity in Munich was substantial, even if the obvious avariciousness of Nazi functionaries meant the NSDAP was not.

In Munich, with rare, notable exceptions, there was little of what could be accurately termed 'resistance' to National Socialist rule. The two most significant acts against the Nazi regime in the city occurred during the war. In the autumn of 1939, Johann Georg Elser (1903-1945), a joiner and former communist from Königsbronn in Bavaria's neighbouring state of Württemberg, planted a bomb in a pillar of the Bürgerbräukeller, ready for Hitler's annual 8 November reunion with his old comrades to commemorate the Nazi dead in the failed 1923 putsch. After speaking for almost an hour, at 9.07pm Hitler left the beer hall early, heavy fog forcing him to return to Berlin by train at

Members of the White Rose: Hans (left) and Sophie Scholl (centre) with Christoph Probst (right)

9.31pm rather than aeroplane. The bomb exploded at 9.20pm, killing eight people and destroying the dais on which Hitler had been standing minutes before. Hitler had narrowly missed death and the war would go on, prompting the Nazi newspaper the *Völkischer Beobachter* to describe it as 'the miraculous salvation of the Führer', perhaps the most accurate words it ever used. Elser was soon picked up by police when attempting to illegally cross the border into Switzerland near Lake Constance. On 5 April 1945, just days before the end of the war, 'on the orders of the Führer' he was taken from the concentration camp at Dachau and killed.

Public perception towards the Nazi regime altered significantly as the successes of the German military froze in the Russian winter of 1942/1943, initially culminating in the colossal defeat at Stalingrad. This coincided with the final months' existence of Munich's most famous anti-Nazi group, the White Rose (Weiße Rose), formed by students Hans Scholl (1918-1943) and Alexander Schmorell (1916/17-1943), joined later by *inter alia* Sophie Scholl (1921-1943), sister of Hans, Christoph Probst (1919-1943), Willy Graf (1918-

1943) and Munich philosophy professor Kurt Huber (1893-1943). Driven by strong Christian beliefs, Hans Scholl, Schmorrel and Graf were horrified by the slaughter they had seen on the Eastern Front. They started printing leaflets condemning the regime, and on 4 February 1942 Sophie even daubed 'Down With Hitler' and 'Freedom!' in huge letters on a wall of the university. On 18 February 1943, Hans and Sophie left leaflets at the university that boldly stated: 'The nation is deeply shaken by the destruction of the men of Stalingrad. The genial strategy of the World War [I] corporal has senselessly and irresponsibly driven 330,000 men to their deaths and ruin. Führer, we thank you!'

Jakob Schmied, a caretaker at the university, spotted the Scholls positioning the leaflets and alerted the Gestapo, an act one Munich historian has recently derided as the 'hour of the power of the small man'. The subsequent Nazi kangaroo court of 22 February at Munich's Justizpalast (Palace of Justice), overseen by the notorious Nazi judge Roland Freisler, inevitably handed out death sentences. Sophie Scholl, 21, and Hans Scholl, 24, along with Christoph Probst, 23, were guillotined the same afternoon.

Terror was a telling factor in dissuading people from opposing National Socialism; but the regime had also acquired a high degree of legitimacy among much of the population, not just in Munich but across the whole of Germany. It would, however, be incorrect to interpret this 'regime legitimacy' as support for Nazi genocidal policies. As Ian Kershaw has posited, the path to the Holocaust was paved with 'a fatal degree of indifference' rather 'than dynamic hatred towards the Jews'.

The persecution of Munich's 9,005 Jews (just 1.2 per cent of the city's 735,388 population) started when 280 were arrested on 9 March 1933. In stages – encompassing employment restrictions to the outlawing of the use of public facilities and the wearing of a yellow star to organised violence – life became increasingly difficult for the city's Jews. Moreover, it was Munich that provided the background to the most significant escalation of persecution of Germany's Jews before the outbreak of the Second World War: the nationwide *Reichskristallnacht* (Night of Broken Glass) of 9–10 November 1938, an anti-Jewish pogrom initiated after a speech by Propaganda Minister Joseph Goebbels (1897-1945) in Munich's Altes Rathaus. Coordinated and set in motion from the city, it left hundreds of German Jews dead (some estimates are 1,000 to 2,000) and saw around 30,000 Jewish men arrested and imprisoned in concentration camps for varying lengths of times. This was arguably the start of a process that ended not in the euphemism of 'protective custody', but in the mass shootings and extermination camps of the Holocaust. In fact, for Munich's Jews, the escalation of violence preceded *Reichskristallnacht*: by June 1938 Hitler had already personally ordered the destruction of the city's main synagogue, on Herzog-Max-Straße. The industrial-scale murder of Europe's Jews was facilitated by war, initially by mass shootings, then in specially constructed death camps in the 'east'. In mid-1939, Munich's Jews numbered 4,535. In 1941 most of them were forced into the 'Jewish Settlement Milbertshofen' (a few kilometres from the city centre), from where, on 20 November 1941, 1,000 were transported to Kaunas, Lithuania, and shot. By February 1945, a total of 3,666 Jews had been deported and murdered. US soldiers found 32,000 surviving but emaciated prisoners in the concentration camp at Dachau on 29 April, and the following day troops counted 80 surviving Jews in Munich.

Chapter 4

A NEW MUNICH (1945-2010)

~

Rebuilding

In 1949, Thomas Mann was finally persuaded to return briefly, with much apprehension and reluctance, to Munich, the city in which he had lived for 40 years, the city with which much of his work was synonymous and the city from which he went into exile after the Nazi takeover of power in 1933. Reflecting on his Munich visit, in October 1949 he wrote from his home in Pacific Palisades, in the USA:

> Certainly Munich came off quite pleasantly and without sour notes. The big press conference; the Academy's reception in the Prinz Karl Palais …; the Goethe lecture; the banquet in the evening at the Rathaus – it all went along nicely and amicably and innocuously, really as if nothing had happened. Whereas the sight of the city was an emphatic reminder of what had happened. To see this whole portion of an outlived past reappearing in a tattered and battered state, with faces of people so much aged, had something ghostly about it, and I did a great deal of looking away.

Today, walking down the wide streets of Munich's Maximilianstraße and Ludwigstraße, or visiting the Altstadt and crossing Marienplatz towards the Frauenkirche or wandering down Tal towards the river Isar, a stranger would be forgiven for getting the impression that Munich's historic buildings and streets had been left untouched by the war. Much, if not quite everything, seems as it ever was. The reality, as Thomas Mann alluded to in his letter, is that the centre of Munich, built up through centuries into one of the most architecturally significant cities in Europe, was little more than rubble by the war's end. Perhaps not quite the mythical *Stunde Null* (zero-hour), but not far from it.
Mann, visiting the city after four years of sporadic rubble clearing and early

US troops remove a sign that reads: 'Capital of the Movement. Munich'

reconstruction efforts, had not seen the city at its nightmarish worst. Munich writer Wilhelm Hausenstein (1882-1957) described his reaction on seeing the city towards the end of the war: 'One stands horrified, horrified and then again horrified.' As the war neared its conclusion, US troops finally entered Munich on 30 April 1945, the same day Hitler shot himself in his Berlin bunker. A week later, on 8 May 1945, Thomas Mann's son Klaus returned to his home city. 'I had imagined it would be terrible,' he wrote lugubriously, 'but it was even worse. Munich no longer exists. The city centre from the main station to Odeonsplatz is composed only of ruins. I could hardly find my way to the English Garden since all the streets that I knew so intimately had become so horribly … disfigured.'

British technological advances, particularly the development of radar, meant Munich had become a realistic target for the Royal Air Force by the summer of 1942. That proved to be just a prelude to the catastrophe to come, and as Richard Bauer argues, German attacks on Warsaw, Rotterdam and numerous industrial cities in Britain had sown the seeds for the destruction o German cities.

Munich suffered around 60 heavy Allied bombing raids between 194. 1945. Though not the utter destruction of some other German cities, a third to a half of all Munich buildings were either completely or heavily destroyed, in the Altstadt around 60 per cent; around the Hauptbahnhof (main station) and Schwabing areas, total destruction was about 70 per cent; across the whole city area, only around two per cent of all buildings were left completely unscathed by Allied attacks; 108 of 206 churches, 40 per cent of administration buildings and 50 per cent of hospitals and schools suffered huge damage. Much of Munich consisted of an estimated five million cubic metres of rubble and in addition to long-standing Munich citizens, it was now also inhabited by a maelstrom of tens of thousands of refugees, forced labourers, displaced persons, the homeless and the formerly persecuted.

As well as destroying buildings and infrastructure, Allied air raids killed 6,373 people from 1942 up to and including 1945. By the end of the war, more than 27,000 residents of the city had been killed either while on military service or through air raids on the city. Though this was only a fraction of the devastation wrought by Nazi aggression on large areas of eastern Europe and and the Soviet Union, it was, nevertheless, devastating for the city and its inhabitants.

Germany was an utterly defeated nation, literally on its knees, at the mercy of the major victorious Allies: Britain, France, the Soviet Union and the USA. The country was split into zones of occupation, with modern-day Bavaria falling under the jurisdiction of the US occupation authority, as did its destroyed capital, Munich. But it was still difficult for some to gauge exactly where the future of the city lay. Hausenstein's drastic suggestion was that perhaps the ruins of Munich should be abandoned and a new city built at another location. 'The fall of the city,' he wrote, 'is basically so radical that I can not imagine a revival.' How wrong he was: over the next six decades, initially under US tutelage, Munich rose out of the proverbial ashes to help construct a deep-seated political culture in Germany that fully embraced democracy and to help play a significant role in the creation of the country's *Wirtschaftswunder* (economic miracle). In light of where Munich – and much of Germany – was in 1945, it is difficult to overstate the scale of this achievement.

The Allies' cumbersome though admirable attempt at the denazification of Germany had many facets. In Munich, around 3,000 city administrators were dismissed for having been members of the NSDAP, while Ritter-v.-Epp-Platz, Adolf-Wagner-Straße and Hermann-Göring-Straße were given back their pre-Nazi-era names of Promenadeplatz, Dahlienstraße and Azaleenstraße respectively. There were also the much-criticised *Fragebogen*, which saw the occupation authorities address individuals with the aim of determining where they stood vis-à-vis Nazism and their guilt – or otherwise – in Nazi crimes. British-Irish writer James Stern (1904-1993) was one of the many people sent to Germany to conduct the *Fragebogen* interviews. A fluent German-speaker, he had spent many years in Germany prior to the Nazi takeover in 1933, before moving for a number of years to the US, in whose military he now served. Stern was less than impressed with the *Fragebogen* the US authorities had provided: '[T]he *Fragebogen*, the questionnaires,' he wrote, 'had been worded, it seemed to me, in the most peculiar German, and I'd put myself in the place of the interviewee and wondered how on earth I myself would answer some of the vague, sometimes unintentionally humorous queries.' It was something many Germans were similarly asking.

Between 5 March 1946, when the Rathaus decreed a law entitled *Befreiung von Nationalsozialismus und Militarismus* (perhaps best translated as Liberation from National Socialism and Militarism), and 1948, of the 29,902 people questioned in Munich, 168 (0.6 per cent) were categorised as 'major offenders'. The number of 'incriminated' totalled 1,462 (4.9 per cent), 'less incriminated' 3,967 (13.3 per cent), 'tacit supporter' 22,847 (76.3 per cent) while 1,458 (4.9 per cent) were deemed 'innocent'. Those deemed guilty enough had to face a *Spruchkammer* (hearing committee), which decided on the sentences to be carried out. One such person was the Nazi ex-mayor of the city, Karl Fiehler. As highlighted by Andreas Heusler, Fiehler, was an 'unrestrained fanatical and racist agitator' and 'one of the most important protagonists of the conception and execution of antisemitic exclusion and persecution measures' against Munich's Jews. The *Spruchkammer* sentenced Fiehler to two years in a work camp but he was immediately freed on account of his already having served three and a half years in a detention camp, while in addition one-fifth of his wealth was confiscated. The mild punishment was, apparently, on account of 'mitigating circumstances' relating to his alleged 'simple-mindedness'.

In truth, denazification was proving to be partly unworkable, for the simple reason that calculating the extent of involvement in the Nazi regime was more a lofty ideal than an easily carried out practical exercise. The dismissal of the 3,000 city administrators meant there were insufficient people to run a hugely destroyed city that was desperately in need of efficient organisation in the form of a well-run bureaucracy. Apart from some major offenders, many were soon re-employed due to sheer expediency.

James Stern, who had found the *Fragebogen* so comical, recorded his experiences of those first few post-war hunger-filled and angst-riddled months in his occasionally condescending but nevertheless illuminating *The Hidden Damage*. Aside from his contempt for the claim from just about everybody he spoke to that they had never supported the Nazi regime, his book is most interesting for his articulation of the profound destruction of Germany's towns and cities. After visiting *inter alia* Frankfurt and Stuttgart, his account provides a vivid contemporary image of the once grand city of Munich. 'The devastation of Munich was different again from other cities,' he wrote. 'The Bavarian capital seemed to have died in a peculiar way, like a handsome woman who has been shot to death many times, but whose skin, hair, eyes and lips have left abundant evidence as to why she was admired.'

Münchners were primarily preoccupied with eking out a living in their war-torn city. Housing, food and fuel were the priorities, but real recoverey required a functioning economy. No different from the rest of what became West Germany, the currency reform of June 1948 was a turning point, providing the catalyst for the *Wirtschaftwunder*, the term used to describe the remarkable transformation of the country's economy and with it the future of the country. In the same year, Thomas Wimmer of the SPD was elected mayor of Munich. Wimmer became hugely popular for his modest, unassuming manner in dealing with the everyday problems facing the population, and he is best remembered for his 'Rama dama', the nickname given to his imaginative citizen-led rubble-clearing initiative, which contributed to the inner city being largely clear of debris by 1950.

The question of the style of Munich's reconstruction was contentious. The leader of Munich's building and planning office, Karl Meitinger, eschewed modern architectural plans, instead favouring either rebuilding the city's ruined historic buildings or replacing them with what can only be described as a kind of 'new-old' style. 'Under all circumstances,' explained Meitinger 'we must strive to save the appearance and the picture of the Altstadt, and preserve what is worthwhile from what is still in existence.' Although Meitinger and his fellow conservatives did not entirely get their own way, the reconstruction of much of the Altstadt as well as many other notable houses, museums and other buildings around the city (today a magnet for tourists and all this implies for the city's economic well-being) is a decision few contemporary Münchners would now take issue with.

In fact, as Gavriel D Rosenfeld in *Munich and Memory* shows, Meitinger's ideas were also a continuation of Munich's architectural traditionalist and anti-modernist predilections, which were most evident in the Weimar era. Post-war, therefore, there was a lot more to this preference for traditional over modern architecture than merely drawing in tourists. Rosenfeld is just one scholar who sees the rebuilding of old buildings as a backward-looking and exculpatory reaction to the city's Nazi past. In short, the result was to shine a rather large light on the city's pre-Nazi role as a *Kunststadt* of world renown. According to Rosenfeld:

> The price of restoring the city's damaged architecture to its pre-war condition, however, was the partial denial of recent history. This was most evident in the inability to mourn the extensive losses caused by the war. By casting away concerns with architectural authenticity, by believing they were allowed to rebuild their destroyed buildings in the same way as the Nazi's primary victims, such as the Poles, traditionalists pursued a programme that – regardless of the degree of intent – tended to deny the historicity of the war as well as German guilt for it.

At least until recent decades, this helped foster the tendency to marginalise the role the city had played in the rise of the Nazis, the city's role as the 'Capital of the Movement' and the city's subsequent destruction.

There is, however, a compelling argument that this has begun to change in recent years. British historian Ian Kershaw first visited Munich in 1972, spent 1976 in the city working at the Institut für Zeitgeschichte on a Third Reich research project and regularly visits the city for research. Kershaw, therefore, has had first-hand experience of the changing nature of the city's relationship

The centrally located Altes Rathaus (left, with road through archway) and the Heilig Geist church (top) were typically little more than shells by the end of the war

with its Nazi past. He explains how on his early visits to Munich he 'went round all the various sites that were associated with Hitler and the Nazis, and there were little overt signs' to suggest a link to the Third Reich. 'There was a little monument to the victims of National Socialism,' he explains 'which, as I recall, was stuck in a car park somewhere off Briennerstraße, but not much else. It was as if every type of reference to the Nazi period had been erased.' Kershaw describes a visit with a Jewish friend to the Bürgerbräukeller, which had been heavily damaged during the war, later rebuilt, before it was finally torn down. He remembers, 'There was a plaque on the wall [with] ... the history of the Burgerbräukeller. What was striking about it was that two dates that were significant in the history of the Bürgerbräukeller – the 1923 Putsch attempt and the 1939 assassination attempt on Hitler [by Georg Elser] both of which were carried out there – were not mentioned. The history of the Bürgebräukeller with two key dates missing.'

This certainly fits in with Rosenfeld's research on Munich's marginalisation of its public memory of its Nazi past. But since Kershaw's introduction to Munich almost 40 years ago, he now sees a city that has started to redress the balance. 'If you go to Briennerstraße,' he points out, 'and the old heartland of the party – to Königsplatz – there are now plaques set up and guides to show where the old Nazi buildings were, right near the Führerbau. So, to that extent, the city has adjusted somewhat.' Without overstating the progress the city has made, two further examples serve to highlight how far the city has come since the early post-war decades. Firstly, 'Chiffren der Erinnerung' is a permanent exhibition at the Stadtmuseum detailing the inextricable relationship between National Socialism and Munich. And, secondly, cited by Kershaw, the construction of the NS-Dokumentationszentrum in München (Munich Documentation Centre for the History of National Socialism, started in 2009) at a location near Königsplatz. Although not universally popular, the Documentation Centre, the earlier work at Königsplatz plus the Stadtmuseum exhibition right next to the superb new Jewish buildings at St.-Jakobs-Platz should all be welcomed as significant steps in the recalibration of the city's memory of its Nazi past.

Left: post-war shoppers queue among the ruins of Munich in sight of the clock tower of the city's Neues Rathaus

Germany's Secret Capital?

The advent of the Cold War saw Germany divided into a capitalist west and communist east, a split synonymous with the wider reality of a bipolar division of many parts of the world. In short, leaders in Washington, London and Paris now saw Germany as a useful bulwark against Russian-led communism. With Berlin likewise divided into capitalist west and communist east, by the 1960s Munich's increasing economic significance and the relocation of many top firms to Bavaria meant it was named by weekly magazine *Der Spiegel* – with a huge sense of irony – as Germany's 'secret capital'. Nevertheless, this represented quite a transformation for what in the early 1950s had been seen – at least industrially and economically – as the capital of the most underdeveloped state in West Germany. Wealth and prosperity attracted increasing numbers of people to the city, and by December 1957 Munich had a population of one million, while the inane – though successful – slogan of *Weltstadt mit Herz*, (cosmopolitan city with a heart), branded the city as a tourist destination to millions. The 1958 Munich air crash, which wiped out much of the Manchester United football team, a further aeroplane crash on Bavariaring in 1960 (leaving 52 dead) and the 1962 Schwabinger Krawalle (Schwabing riots) were low points in an otherwise upward trajectory for the reputation of the city since 1945.

Within Munich, many of the plaudits for the city's rise from destruction were handed to the social democrat-run city administration led until 1960 by Mayor Thomas Wimmer. In the Munich local elections of 1948, Wimmer's SPD had won 15 of 50 seats, beating the incumbent Christian Social Union (CSU, Christlich-

Der Spiegel declares Munich 'Germany's secret capital'

Soziale Union, a conservative party exclusive to Bavaria), which won 10 seats, to become the largest party on the all-important city council, and with it ensuring the city's first social democratic mayor since 1924. The Bavaria Party (BP, Bayernpartei), described by Graham Ford as 'an extreme particularist party, advocating an extreme form of federalism', took many CSU votes when winning 13 seats. In the mayoral election, Karl Scharnagl, the CSU incumbent, had been somewhat sidelined after being the centre of newspaper allegations about his having a predilection for nude bathing clubs, and Wimmer easily won the vote (at this time mayors were elected by the city council). In the following local elections of 1952, the first in which Munich's population directly voted not only for the party but also for the mayor, the SPD won the largest share of seats (25 of 60), while Wimmer won a convincing 60.9 per cent of the mayoral vote. Even with Munich's housing problems reaching crisis point, Wimmer still managed a final election triumph in 1956 (the SPD won 28 of 60 seats to the CSU's 16), when he won a commendable 58.3 per cent.

Future Munich mayor Hans-Jochen Vogel (right) learns how to carry out the Oktoberfest *Anzapf'n* from the current mayor, Thomas Wimmer (left)

But there was a tangible feeling in the city that Munich required a new direction, new leadership; indeed, the *Münchner Merkur* newspaper had already reported on 30 November 1955 that Wimmer was struggling to hold the city council together. In 1960, 73-year-old Wimmer stepped aside in favour of the manifestly younger 34-year-old Hans-Jochen Vogel, who won that year's mayoral contest with 64.3 per cent of the vote, his SPD winning 53.4 per cent. Vogel was as much an intellectual as Wimmer was a man of the people (indeed, it was Wimmer who introduced the ritual *Anzapf'n*, the very public mayoral opening of the first Oktoberfest barrel of beer that kicks off the – usually – 16-

Britain's Queen Elizabeth II's 1962 visit to Munich

day festival), and he proved to be every bit as popular. With an increasingly successful economy, the once again self-proclaimed art metropolis also established itself as West Germany's film and television capital. And in 1962, with Berlin somewhat indisposed, Vogel laid out the red carpet for France's President Charles de Gaulle and in 1965 for Britain's Queen Elizabeth II. After a landslide victory in Munich's local elections of 1966, the SPD (with 58.4 per cent), again led by Vogel (who won a never-to-be-repeated 78 per cent), now held a similar dominance in Munich that the conservative CSU held throughout much of the rest of Bavaria: with a CSU interlude between 1978 and 1984, the SPD has ruled alone or in a coalition in Munich since Wimmer's 1948 victory; similarly, with the exception of 1954 to 1957, the CSU has governed the federal state of Bavaria since 1945, for much of that time with an overall majority.

On the back of its economic prosperity, Munich's population was growing rapidly, gaining 300,000 people between 1960 and 1972 to reach 1.34 million. In addition, in 1962 Munich's 100,000th so-called – and pejoratively at that – 'guest-worker' (initially from Italy, then Spain, Greece and Turkey) arrived. In the same period, around 175,000 houses or apartments were built (a huge number but nowhere near solving the city's ongoing chronic housing shortage), and 1,770 school places and more than 2,800 hospital beds were created, while the Altstadt was pedestrianised for good measure. At the same time, Munich was becoming a car-owning city: in 1950, there were 77 motor vehicles per 1,000 inhabitants; by 1960 this ratio had more than doubled and by 2008 the number had soared to 501 per 1,000 inhabitants. A total of 420 kilometres of rail transport was constructed in order to begin the necessary connections for new and old settlements within the city, principally on the back of the 1966 decision by the International Olympic Committee to award the 1972 Olympic Games to Munich. Considering that 30 years earlier, the 1936 Berlin Olympics had been indelibly tainted as the 'Nazi Games', and what was a mere 21 years after the fall of the Third Reich, this was a momentous decision.

By the time of the opening ceremony for the 1972 Olympics, Munich had 16 kilometres of U-Bahn (underground) and 17 accompanying stations, plus an architectural jewel in its Olympic stadium, which arguably proved to be much bolder in design than any other modern construction in the city. The stage was set for a great Olympics in a flourishing city; but the attack by radical Palestinians that left 17 dead cast a further dark shadow over the city's name. In light of Munich's central role in the establishment of the Third Reich, the fact that most of the victims of the attack were Israeli athletes could do nothing but compound the scale of the tragedy. Munich was once again the centre of the world's attention, once again portrayed on television screens across the world in a negative light.

Vogel's decision not to run again for mayor, however, was related to the much more mundane matter of SPD fratricidal in-fighting, though he successfully went on to serve as a German cabinet minister under the SPD chancellorship of Helmut Schmidt and also to serve for a short time as mayor of Berlin. His successor in the Munich hot seat was Georg Kronawitter, the 44-year-old son of a farmer and an agriculture expert, who won 55.9 per cent of the vote in the 1972 Munich elections to prolong the SPD's dominance in the Rathaus. Though Kronawitter's SPD won 52.7 per cent of city's vote, internal squabbling between the far left and centre was beginning to take its toll on the party, reflected in the drop of more than 5 per cent from the previous election. Even though he continued to have the support of much of the population, it was no surprise that Kronawitter decided not to seek re-election in 1978. The left-wing SPD mayoral candidate, Max von Heckel, a thorn in Kronawitter's side, proceeded to blow the 1978 election, meaning the CSU could celebrate not only holding the reins of power across Bavaria, but also in the capital.

If much of Bavaria seemed to have a fascination with the CSU of almost one-party state proportions, it seems that the population of Munich realised too late that it could not stomach a CSU mayor. To be fair to the new mayor, Erich Kiesl, with economic stagnation across Europe, it was not a great time to be the first CSU office holder in Munich since Karl Scharnagl in 1948. Though a moderate conservative, his involvement in a stream of half-scandals and misdemeanours, hastily pounced upon by a generally hostile local press, did little to help his cause. Splashing out on a costly renovation of the mayoral office, rising expense allowances, a comical and costly attempt to create a Münchener Filmwoche (Munich Film Week) and employing an assistant for his wife were serious enough but hardly likely to make the political sky fall in. Nevertheless, Kiesl had gained a reputation in the press for being 'superficial' and 'arrogant' with it.

While Kiesl was struggling to convince Munich that he was worthy of his mayoral robes, the city once again caught the world's attention for the wrong reasons when on 26 September 1980 a right-wing extremist exploded a bomb at the Oktoberfest, killing himself and a further 12 people, and injuring a further 219. With the murder of the Israeli athletes during the Munich Olympics, echoes of Nazism seemed intent on jolting the city in spectacularly tragic ways.

The creation of Munich's department of the environment in 1981, well in advance of most other cities around the world, although forward-thinking, has not saved Kiesl's reputation as one of the lesser lights in the line-up of post-war Munich mayors. Allegations of the selling of land at a knock-down price dogged his 1984 mayoral election efforts, ensuring that the lack of affordable housing was a central feature of the 1984 local election campaign, with the SPD claiming that '400,000 tenants are more important to us that a handful of property tycoons and speculators,' In a run-off with a rejuvenated Kronawitter (the first vote had not secured a majority for any mayoral candidate), Kiesl was decisively defeated, gaining only 41.9 per cent of the vote in a two-horse race.

Kronawitter aside, the SPD 1984 local election victory was far from convincing: the party managed just 41.9 per cent (33 of 80 seats), fewer votes than the CSU (42.4 per cent and 35 seats), heralding change as the SPD chose to

In the last decades of the 20th century, Westpark and Nordpark joined the English Garden (above) as popular green city spaces

govern in coalition with the rising Green party (Die Grünen), which had won six seats. The same red-green political configuration has ruled the city ever since (following elections in 1990, 1996, 2002 and 2008).

By 1989/90, the national political environment had changed beyond recognition as the Berlin Wall fell and Germany was reunified. Munich had more than 5,000 visitors from East Germany as early as 9 to 10 November 1989, just hours after the opening of the Berlin Wall, but as is now abundantly clear the end of the Cold War and German reunification involved huge economic and social dislocations, challenges that play a significant role in the country to the present day. With Berlin reunified, and in 2000 once again the capital of Germany, Munich lost its spurious claim to be Germany's 'secret capital': it also seemed set to lose out to Berlin's claim to be Germany's so-called 'capital of culture'. By 1990, Berlin was attracting a greater number of tourists than Munich, while the Munich-based *Süddeutsche Zeitung* proclaimed 'Munich's New Mediocrity'. Few observers went out of their way to strongly demur.

In the spring of 1991, an announcement that the city had to make savings of

100 to 150 million marks engendered deep-felt animosity between the CSU-run Bavarian government and the SPD-led Munich city council. The reality, however, was that Munich was suffering, but doing rather better than most other cities in Germany. At between 3 and 4 per cent, Munich had the lowest level of unemployment for any city in Germany, and with it the city had the lowest debt by a large margin of Germany's ten largest cities. Moreover, during Kronawittter's terms in office, Munich saw a substantial increase in the amount of green spaces created, notably with Westpark and Nordpark, the building of the Gasteig cultural centre (though massively over budget), the renovation of the Muffathalle to become a cutting-edge concert and exhibition centre and the construction of the marvellous Literaturhaus, something of a centre point for authors and journalists in Europe's largest publishing city.

In 1993, Kronawitter announced his intention not to stand for mayor in the forthcoming Munich elections, paving the way for his SPD colleague Christian Ude's first of a remarkable four (1993, 1999, 2002 and 2008) consecutive election victories. Around the same time, it became much more widely acknowledged that all that was happening in Berlin was not quite the runaway success envisaged in the wake of the opening of the Berlin Wall and German reunification: the city had – and has – huge economic problems, the realisation of which, a touch perversely, provided Munich with a fillip to its sulking pride. Press releases once again started to emerge from the city's cultural affairs department proclaiming Munich as Germany's capital of culture. It had not taken long.

The immediate post-war years had been ones of austerity, but the *Wirtschaftswunder* fundamentally transformed Bavaria. No other city in Bavaria represented this transformation more than Munich: once seen as capital of the most underdeveloped state in Germany, today it is the centre of Germany's 'high-tech industry' and for many the country's most sought-after place to live.

PART 2
THE PATH TO MODERNITY

For centuries Marienplatz was Munich's most important marketplace
(watercolour by Carl Friedrich Heinzmann, 1836)

Chapter 5

INDUSTRY, ECONOMY AND INNOVATION

~

In The Beginning

In the beginning ... there was salt. Salt – or 'white gold' – was until as late as the 19th century vitally important as a food preservative, and was one of the principal reasons Heinrich der Löwe established his settlement on the Isar in the 1150s. As early as 1195, sources refer to the existence of traders in Munich, and in the 13th century the existence of a hospital (north of today's Viktualienmarkt) is recorded, while a Regensburg document of 1229 refers to a Jewish settlement in Munich, the inhabitants of which were given legal status in 1315. These, plus a growing population, all testify to a flourishing city by the early 14th century. In addition to the lucrative salt trade, the river Isar proved a useful, if somewhat hazardous, transportation route for the trading of wood. These two commodities received the royal stamp of approval in the 14th century when it was decreed that both salt and wood had to be stored in Munich before being moved elsewhere for sale, consequently providing Munich with huge long-term economic gains.

With salt as a mainstay, and with its own mint, Munich soon became a regional centre for the trading of cloth, wine from South Tyrol and even rudimentary banking, all of which helped keep Munich's patrician class in considerable wealth. And as a leading regional centre, with strong connections to Austria, meat, fish, bread, cereals, spices and wines were widely available at various weekly markets in the city, the biggest and most important of which was the central Marktplatz, today's Marienplatz (which, in fine medieval style, was also the location for periodic jousting tournaments and other cultural events). In addition, farmers – or just about anybody with a patch of soil to grow on – in and around the city grew crops, primarily for their own consumption, unless, in an occasional good year, they had a surplus to sell at market for profit. To place the city into a wider context at this time, flourishing though Munich undoubtedly was (including the highest tax revenue in Upper Bavaria) by the mid-14th century, it could not be compared to the much more important and much wealthier cities of Regensburg, Augsburg and Nuremberg, all of which were southern trading and political centres of European import.

Salt continued to be an important mainstay of the prosperity of Munich, even after the city's patrician-led monopoly on its trade ended and was replaced by a royal monopoly in 1587, when Wilhelm V in effect nationalised it. Though undoubtedly a setback to the economic prosperity of some of the city's leading families, increasing employment by the royal court in Munich slightly softened the blow. While in 1500 only 162 of Munich's 13,500 population were employed by the royal court, the number had leapt to over 800 (in a population of 20,000) under Wilhelm V around 80 years later. Parallel to this, the unification of Upper and Lower Bavaria under Duke Albrecht IV in 1503 meant that the royal court relied to a lesser degree on the economy of Munich and focused to a greater extent on the whole of Bavaria. The other side of the coin was that at a time when Munich was to a diminishing degree the main source of tax revenue for the duke, the city was evolving as the centre of a more efficient bureaucracy for wider Bavaria.

The Thirty Years War, the occupation of Munich by Swedish troops and the subsequent drop in population from around 20,000 in 1620 to below 15,000 in 1650 left Munich with huge economic problems. Particularly hard hit was the city's once thriving textile industry, which lost almost half of its workers. With the support of wealthy backers, various attempts at placing the Munich and the wider Bavarian economy on a more competitive footing were attempted in the next 100 years, most noticeably with the establishment of manufacturers of silver and gold wire, mirrors, leather goods and a range of textile businesses. In the long term, most successful of these operations was the creation of a porcelain manufactory in the Au area of the city, which was relocated to Schloss Nymphenburg in 1761, and which flourishes to this day as Porzellan Manufaktur Nymphenburg, serving an exclusive clientele with high-end porcelain goods, designed by some of the world's most famous designers (Viviane Westwood, Christian Lacroix and Gareth Pugh contributed designs to the company's 260th anniversary in 2008). Few of the newly set-up business projects succeeded for long, and certainly none on a scale large enough to provide a paradigm change in Munich's economic trajectory, exemplified by the continued predominance of modest crafts and trades.

Work by British designer Vivienne Westwood to celebrate 260 years of porcelain manufacturing at Nymphenburg

On the eve of the French Revolution in 1789, Munich had a relatively low percentage of its population engaged in industry, and, as befitting a royal capital with an expanding court, sector specialisation often revolved around luxury goods. As Markus A Denzel has shown, 'Although factories and manufactories could be found in Munich, it was still not a real factory city.' Instead, and above all, one would find 'fancy or fashionable goods shops' as well as a number of bookshops. Of particular importance to the Munich economy were the countless markets that permeated the Munich calendar, the biggest and most important being the Dreikönig and the Jacobi, both coming under the rubric of Dult, or 'fair' in English. Today, the huge Auer Dult takes place three times a year at Mariahilfsplatz and is frequented by tens of thousands of visitors, attracted to the market stalls of every description offering anything from household goods to paintings as well as from countless impressive second-hand bookstalls to traditional food stalls. Just as it had been 400 years before, at the end of the 18th century the Saturday market at Marienplatz continued to be the most important of the regular markets in Munich, attracting visitors from across Bavaria and often further afield.

By the time Napoleon had seized control of the French republic and started on a series of conquests that were to profoundly change the face of Europe, Munich, though no economic pigmy, was in a sense still something of an economic backwater. There were, however, stirrings that pointed the way to a more technical- and innovation-oriented future for the city, led by a number of protagonists, four of whom will be considered below: Joseph von Fraunhofer, Max von Pettenkofer, Carl von Linde and Oskar von Miller.

Joseph von Fraunhofer

Joseph von Fraunhofer (1787-1826) was born into a modest glass-making family in Straubing, south-east of Regensburg, and he was alive during one of Europe's most tumultuous epochs since the Thirty Years War. Both Fraunhofer's parents had died by 1798, and he was sent to live with Philipp Weichselberger, court mirror maker with a workshop in the centre of Munich and glass cutter to the Residenz. An apprenticeship and a modest career in glass beckoned for Fraunhofer, until a stroke of luck intervened.

Future King Maximilian I oversees the rescue of the young Joseph Fraunhofer

Bavaria was, of course, at this time in thrall to Napoleon Bonaparte. In 1801, the French ordered a geographical survey of the whole of Bavaria, which was headed by Joseph von Utzschneider (1763-1840). In the same year, a Munich building collapsed and of 42 people, the only survivors were Weichselberger, his wife and 14-year-old Joseph Fraunhofer. Incredible as it seems, Elector Maximilan Joseph and Utzschneider were on hand to direct the rescue operation, marking a confluence of unfortunate and fortunate events that set Fraunhofer on the path to pre-eminence as one of Europe's foremost scientists. In short, Utzschneider took Fraunhofer under his wing and within eight years he had gone from apprentice to influential co-owner of Utzschneider's company.

Fraunhofer's rise was very much predicated on the context of the time: in October 1805, French troops rescued Munich from Austrian occupation and around a week later Napoleon made his triumphant entrance into the city. The seal on Franco-Bavarian cooperation was provided in 1806 when Napoleon raised Bavaria from an electorate to a kingdom, meaning Maximilian, who had overseen Fraunhofer's rescue, became Bavaria's first king. The French economic blockade of Great Britain after the Battle of Trafalgar in 1806 meant that British precision instruments, at the time considered to be the best in the world, could not be imported for Utzschneider's geographical survey of Bavaria. In 1807, Utzschneider's 22-year-old protégé, Fraunhofer, took over the leadership of the attempt to build the necessary measuring instruments. Not only did Fraunhofer spectacularly succeed at this, he went on to build by far the most accurate telescopes, binoculars, microscopes and magnifying glasses available in the world, easily surpassing those produced in Britain. From this start, Fraunhofer's career took off: at the Mathematical and Mechanical Institute at nearby Benediktbeuren (around 70 kilometres south of Munich), co-owned by Utzschneider and engineer Georg von Reichenbach (1772-1826), Fraunhofer improved production facilities, solved the problem of producing glass without streaks and standardised the process of finishing glass to a previously unheard of high standard. Among a host of developments in the construction of telescopes, Fraunhofer's nine-inch parallactic refractor was vital in enabling Johann Gottfried Galle (1812-1910) to discover the planet Neptune in 1846. In addition, although Fraunhofer was not the first scientist to discover the more than 500 dark lines in the Sun's spectrum, which are now known as Fraunhofer Lines, he was the first to understand their importance and act on their significance.

Today, Fraunhofer's name lives on in the Munich-based Fraunhofer-Gesellschaft, a world-class research institute. He was widely recognised as a pioneer, and it was on the back of his achievements that Bavaria became the world leader in optics and precision instruments, though only for a short time. His death in 1826, at just 39, most likely poisoned from his years of scientific experiments, doused any pretensions Munich had of becoming a genuine centre of innovation and of modern research. That Fraunhofer took most of his work secrets with him to his grave hardly helped his Munich successors.

Modernisation & Industrialisation

Munich's modernisation under the reign of King Maximilian I and his First Minister Maximilian Joseph von Montgelas during the Napoleonic era was a natural corollary to wider Bavarian modernisation. With huge debts caused by the wars, climbing to more than 200 million gulden by 1815, Montgelas had considerable difficulties in constructing the desired efficient bureaucratic state apparatus that would provide a basis on which to build a modern economy. The most notable reforms included the final abolition of serfdom, secularisation, the nationalisation of the postal system, the abolition of inner-Bavarian tolls and tax reforms. However, the difficulty for Bavaria was that while some countries had already set out on a path of industrialisation (most obviously Great Britain, arguably since around the 1780s), similar developments in Bavaria (such as innovations in textiles, developments in steam power or iron production that typically drove the Industrial Revolution) were negligible.

In addition, Maximilian I's successor, Ludwig I, was much more preoccupied in raising Munich to a city renowned for its art and culture, and his accession to the Bavarian throne in 1825 probably did more harm than good to the prospects of Munich's rapid industrialisation. Nevertheless, it was under Ludwig's reign that the university at Landshut (actually founded in Ingolstadt in 1472, moving to Landshut only in 1800) was transferred to Munich in 1826, that a customs union was created with Württemberg, then with the rest of the German Confederation in 1834, Bavaria's first railway lines were constructed and the Munich stock exchange came into existence, while Ludwig himself promoted various industrial exhibitions, principally in Munich.

Ludwig's fall in the wake of the Lola Montez affair of 1848, which saw the accession of Maximilian II, opened the door for a modest quickening of modernisation. Press censorship was relaxed, the Maximilianeum, at that time an elite school, was erected at the end of Maximilianstraße, while the expansion of the city's borders meant that the Altstadt started to become less of a desirable place to live in, resulting in fewer dwellings and more banks, businesses and, reflecting the greater role beer played in the city's economy, more beer halls. Moreover, the reform of the judiciary, the extension of railway lines (Berlin, Bodensee and Salzburg were reachable by 1860) and the erection of a network of telegraph lines are further indications of the city's modernisation. In 1817

Munich's population stood at 40,683, by 1850 it had reached 89,000 and by 1869 a huge leap to 159,000 meant that Munich was now the third largest city in Germany, after Berlin and Hamburg. By 1848 there were 92 places of work in Munich large enough to be labelled a 'factory'. These employed, however, a meagre 2,186 people. Significantly, of the 92 factories, 33 were breweries. The food and drink industry as well as clothing manufacturers played an increasingly important role in the city's economy, and still largely predicated on the demands of the royal court, shoemakers, jewellers, goldsmiths and tailors were kept busy. In addition, metal, construction and wood industries grew in importance, particularly on the back of the construction of, for example, the suburb of Maxvorstadt (began 1809), and grand streets such as Ludwigstraße (from the Feldherrnhalle to Siegestor, principally between 1816-1829) and Maximilianstraße (1851-1874). The 1853 Schrannenhalle grain storage facility in the city centre and the rather larger Glaspalast exhibition hall of 1854 were both constructed out of glass and steel, and provided a portent of modern construction projects to come.

In 1837, backed by some of the city's wealthiest traders and bankers, Joseph Anton von Maffei founded in Munich Bavaria's first locomotive factory. Maffei's timing proved to be prescient as he was the right person at the right time when Europe's railway boom took off in the 1840s. By 1849 he had sold a total of 56 locomotives, though not without having weathered fierce financial difficulties, highlighting, according to Margarate Wagner-Braun, 'how difficult it was in mid-century for many Bavarian entrepreneurs to get finance for large-scale investments'. Nevertheless, in 1864 Maffei's employees could celebrate the completion of the company's 500th locomotive, and by 1874, with the additional boost of the creation of the Krauss locomotive company in 1866, Munich had became one of Germany's most important railway centres: one fifth of all Munich companies employing more than 500 people worked in some way in the railway industry at this time.

Moreover, machine factories and the railways were beginning to propel Munich further ahead of Bavarian competitor cities such as Augsburg as the centre of the Bavarian economy. Along with the railways and small- and medium-sized machine factories, breweries also started to play a much more significant role in Munich's economic development, and it was in the latter half of the 19th century that the city gained a reputation as a 'beer city'. The transforma-

By the middle of the19th century, Munich was the centre of locomotive building in Bavaria; in just a few decades, the city's Maffei works became one of the most important in the German Empire (by Friedrich Perlberg, 1882)

tion of Munich's breweries owed much to modern industrial innovations and technologies, such as Carl von Linde's refrigeration machines, as well as better transport infrastructure (the railways enabled beer to be sent further afield, with annual production jumping from 200,000 to 500,000 hectolitres within a decade), while rationalisation inevitably meant that larger brewers bought out smaller firms or smaller concerns simply went to the wall in the heat of economic competition. By the final decades of the century, some of Munich's most recognisable names in the brewing industry were already winning the fight for the lion's share of the trade, for example Paulaner, Pschorr, Hacker, Franziskaner, Löwen and Spaten.

The rise of Munich's brewing industry, however, was predicated on a further vital development: it was reliant on the copious availability of clean water, something that had been far from the case until later decades of the 19th century. The numerous *Bäche* (streams) that circumvented and passed through the centre of Munich (now largely hidden below ground level) had always played a fundamental role in the lives of the city's inhabitants. As well as providing drinking water and a convenient 'sewerage system', the population had a ready supply of water to douse the many fires that broke out in the city. Therefore, the water coursing through the city was an intrinsic part of the economy: it powered water mills for corn and saws for cutting wood, and it was used at mills for grounding spices and for powering smithies. With a plentiful supply of water, butchers, leather goods makers, cloth makers and many other small-scale producers settled near one stream or another, reaching a high point in the middle of the 19th century when around 150 businesses were working aside the city's *Bäche*. The importance of water to Munich's history is today recognised in a number of streets: *Kanal*straße ('canal'), *Quellen*straße ('source of water'), *Lederer*straße ('leather') and *Brunn*straße ('water well'). Of course, the drawback of so many valuable uses of the city's streams was that as people found ever-greater inventive ways to use them, pollution increasingly became a concern, eventually posing a real health hazard to the population.

As in most European cities, as industrialisation expanded, Munich's growing population found itself beset with health problems manifested not only by endemic unhygienic living conditions but also inadequate supplies of clean water. Indeed, in the 1600s, the city council's answer to the all-too frequent plagues of rats had been to offer a reward of one pfennig for every rat killed. And it is not difficult to guess where Münchners were ordered to dispatch the plague-carrying rats: straight into the Isar.

By the mid-19th century, the city was hit by two terrifying outbreaks of cholera: first, in 1836, which killed around 3,000 of the 6,000 affected and propelled thousands of Munich's wealthier citizens to flee. By the time a second significant epidemic hit the city (and much of the Continent), in 1854, some of the best scientific brains in Europe were engaged in a struggle to pinpoint its cause and come up with a way of combating its deadly threat.

Max von Pettenkofer

The doyen of Munich scientific life when the second cholera epidemic struck was the hugely admired Max von Pettenkofer, who, among a host of other prestigious positions, was personal physician at Munich's royal court between 1850 and 1896.

Pettenkofer was born on 3 December 1818 in the small Bavarian town of Lichtenheim, but he was soon bundled off to live in Munich in order to get a good education. There, he lived with his uncle Franz Xaver Pettenkofer, head pharmacist to the Munich Residenz. Pettenkofer studied pharmacy between 1837 and 1843, during which time he caused a stir within the scientific community by developing a forensic method of detecting arsenic, which he successfully demonstrated on a corpse in a criminal case. In 1847 he was appointed Professor of Pathological-Chemical Examinations at the University of Munich and in 1850 he was given a seat on the Bavarian Interior Ministry's medical advisory board.

In a similar vein to Benjamin Thompson in the late 18th century, Pettenkofer proved to be a master of much more than his own field. In 1849, he created a type of cement that was equal in quality to the English Portland cement, which was seen as the best in the world. He came to the attention of King Ludwig I by proving that the deterioration of court oil paintings was due to the use of a varnish (though his efforts at restoration are today viewed with a greater degree of scepticism). And in 1851, he turned his hand to producing a type of gas made from wood, which was subsequently used across southern Germany for gas lighting. By the mid-1850s, therefore, at a time when the scourge of cholera was intermittently sweeping across Europe, killing thousands and scaring the living daylights out of countless more, Pettenkofer was the star of Munich and Bavarian science, a name revered in the European scientific community.

Pettenkofer's greatest achievement was, however, something of a cholera paradox: in his 'soil theory', he came up with a scientific explanation for the cause of cholera that was – as became clear – patently inaccurate. What is more, even when Robert Koch (1843-1910) had, by 1883, proven without too much doubt that he, not Pettenkofer, had found the true cause of cholera, Pettenkofer clung on to his theory in the vain belief it was correct. No, Pettenkofer did not discover the cause of cholera, but while failing to do so he revolutionised the conception of public health and hygiene, and changed the nature of European cities, starting with Munich.

In short, Pettenkofer's soil theory, published in 1855, posited that cholera was not contagious and was transmitted through soil contaminated by the inadequate disposal of human excrement. The logic of this for Pettenkofer was to cleanse the city's soil and with it wipe out cholera, which meant ensuring that the city had sufficient clean water for everyday use and an efficient sewerage system. A new sewerage system was started in 1874 and a clean water supply from the area of Mangfalltal (around 60 kilometres to the south) was available for the first time in 1890, which is today the source of around 80 per cent of Munich's water supply. The result was that by 1900, cholera had been eradicated from the city and typhus deaths had dropped from 407 in 1870 to 25 in 1900.

By the end of the 19th century, Pettenkofer's efforts had transformed Munich in a way unimaginable just decades earlier, and in 1895, Adolf von Hildebrand's neoclassical Wittelsbach Fountain was inaugurated at Lenbachplatz to celebrate Munich's Mangfalltal freshwater supply and new drainage system. From being a city that in mid-century was considered a 'typhus nest' and regarded by some as one of the most unhygienic cities in Europe, a place about which foreign newspapers published warnings regarding its unsanitary conditions, by 1900 Munich had been transformed into a model of hygiene that other cities aspired to. Moreover, Pettenkofer's promotion of public health – encompassing a focus on the quality of air, water and soil, an attention to room ventilation and the necessity of adequate clothing, plus his overall view of cleanliness in the home and his linking of hygiene and health to a successful economy – means that he is considered by many experts to be the 'father of modern hygienic science'.

The success in Munich and the widespread admiration he garnered, however, was not enough for the proud Pettenkofer. When Robert Koch proved that cholera was, in fact, passed from person to person through human excrement and through contaminated drinking water, Pettenkofer obstinately refused to believe his soil theory was incorrect.

Increasingly desperate to prove that cholera could not be passed through drinking water, in 1892 Pettenkofer proceeded with a reckless experiment: he proposed to drink a concoction containing cholera. 'I am 74 years old,' he wrote, in a fit of melancholy, 'I no longer have any teeth … and I feel the burden of my years.' He went on to explain that he did not mind laying down his life in the cause of science, and that if his experiment became life threatening, 'I would face death quietly.'

Though he became only mildly ill, possibly because, as rumoured, an assistant had watered down the potion, or he was just extremely lucky, Pettenkofer survived. But neither this minor 'success' nor a series of prestigious awards from around the world for his work on hygiene could conceal his disillusionment. On the night of 10 February 1901, aged 83, he shot himself dead with a pistol in his Munich apartment.

Carl von Linde

If Joseph von Fraunhofer was Munich's first proto-scientist-entrepreneur, and Max von Pettenkofer was more of an academic-scientist with a less-developed interest in reaping financial rewards via marketing and industry, Carl von Linde managed striking success in both the academic and the business world: he combined brilliance as an academic with an eye for innovation in the market place and, in the process, in Linde, founded what today is one of Germany's biggest companies.

Born in 1842 in Berndorf, Upper Franconia, Carl Linde emerged into a Bavaria that was on the cusp of change. Between 1818 and 1910 the total population of the kingdom of Bavaria grew by 90 per cent: from 3.7 million in 1818 to 4.5 million in 1852 and to five million in 1875, with the principal rises in the cities of Nuremberg, Augsburg and Munich. Between 1871 and 1913, Munich's population increased almost four-fold, from 170,00 to 620,000. This rise in population paralleled the rise of Munich as a renowned centre of brewing, which was predicated on clean water supplies and refrigeration technology. Though Linde did not invent refrigeration, he recognised, in his own understated words, that 'here was an area of mechanical thermodynamics that had not yet been fully explored.' In short, Linde transformed the area of food preservation. What had first been preserved with salt and with ice, both of which had to be sourced and transported, could now be preserved with modern refrigeration technology.

Carl Linde's career should be seen in the wider context of Germany's rise to become the most dynamic economy in Europe by 1914. Under the steam of entrepreneurs, scientists and industrialists, and on the back of a rapidly expanding working class, the German Empire emerged with staggering rapidity not only to be a serious rival to British economic dominance, but by 1914 to be level with Britain and often leading the world in many major industrial indicators: in 1871 Germany produced just 37,900 metric tons of coal to

Britain's 118,000 tons, while by 1913 Germany produced 279,000 to Britain's 292,000; in 1870, Germany produced 1,391 tons of pig iron to Britain's 6,060 tons, while in 1910 it was 14,793 to 10,380 in favour of Germany; and the 1870 figures for steel production show that Germany produced 169 tons to Britain's 286 tons, while in 1910 Germany produced a huge 13,698 tons, more than double Britain's 6,374.

Moreover, Germany was also on its way to becoming the 'world's chemist' and 11 Nobel Prizes were won by German scientists in chemistry and physics between 1901 and 1915, while German universities and technical schools were becoming favoured by the world's brightest students. One of these, the Munich Polytechnic School (now the Technische Universität München), is inextricably linked to the career of Carl von Linde, who became a professor there in 1868.

In 1870/71 Linde published papers in the *Bavarian Industry and Trade Journal* about his highly successful refrigeration experiments. Brewers, who had thus far relied on ice, sometimes transported hundreds of kilometres, to keep beer at a drinkable temperature, were immediately interested in Linde's work. Austrian brewer August Deiglmayer along with Munich brewer Gabriel Sedlmayr were most eager and helped Linde set up an experimental refrigeration machine in Sedlmayr's Munich Spaten brewery. The test was impressive enough for Linde to win a commission to install a refrigeration machine at the Dreher brewery in Trieste, Austria (now part of Italy). Though a reliable version proved to be initially elusive, a much-improved refrigeration machine was installed at Dreher in 1877. Later in the year, the Rotterdam-based Heineken brewery ordered a machine and Carlsberg of Copenhagen followed in 1878. Realising the business potential of his work, and to allow him to concentrate on improving and marketing his machines, in 1878 Linde set up the Gesellschaft für Linde's Eismachinen A.G., and a year later left his university position in Munich for Wiesbaden, the home of his new firm. For all Linde's business acumen, he still did not want to tie himself exclusively to the business world and he returned to Munich in 1890 as an honorary professor, teaching from 1892 onwards. While many of Linde's business competitors did not survive the cyclical ups and downs of the German economy, his company went from strength to strength, even after he left the board in order concentrate almost exclusively on further scientific research. By 1890, Linde's company had de-

livered around 1,000 refrigeration machines to a number of countries, with orders ranging from slaughter houses and ice factories to dairies and chocolate factories. By 1915, his company had sold more than 9,000 machines.
There were a mulititude of reasons for Carl von Linde's success, ranging from his skill as an entrepreneur to his exceptional talent as a scientist. A further key element, however, was that he preferred to employ people he knew and could rely upon, which often entailed using graduates from his own Munich university. Although the Linde headquarters remained for many years in Wiesbaden, the company is today based in Munich, employs tens of thousands of people across the world and still has a close relationship with the Technische Universität München. By his death in 1934, Linde had been one of only a handful of people who had managed to successfully marry academia and business in a manner that is still relatively unusual today.

Oskar von Miller & the Deutsches Museum

While art lovers have a plethora of galleries and museums to choose from around the city, with more than a million visitors every year the Deutsches Museum is by far the most frequented museum not just in Munich but in Germany; and regarding quality, it compares fantastically well with the world's best science and technology museums, for example La Cité des Sciences in Paris, the Science Museum and the Natural History Museum, both in London, Washington's Natural History Museum and Chicago's Museum of Science and Industry.
The current director of the Deutsches Museum is Wolfgang Heckl, a renowned physicist, who has worked at various institutes, including under Nobel Prize winner Theodor W Hänsch at Munich's Max Planck Institute of Quantum Optics. He also studied under Nobel Prize winner Professor Gerd Billig. Heckl's role at the Deutsches Museum is complemented by his role as professor of experimental physics at the Ludwig-Maximilians-Universität-München.
In taking on the role of director of the Deutsches Museum, Heckl was following in the footsteps of Oskar von Miller (1855-1934), the driving force behind the creation of the museum. Miller was the youngest son of Ferdinand von Miller (1813-1887), Munich's great metal-founder, famous for cast-

Oskar von Miller,
founder of the Deutsches Museum

ing the huge Bavaria statue that stands on Theresienwiese. After studying civil engineering, Oskar von Miller joined the Bavarian civil service, and in 1881 he was sent to an exhibition in Paris displaying electrical engineering, which inspired him to successfully put on his own demonstration of how electricity could be carried long-distances, in this case from Munich to Miesbach. In 1883 he moved to Berlin in order to work for the German Edison Company, before returning to Munich in 1889 to found his own engineering consultancy firm, with which he secured his reputation over the next 30 years as an innovator with various practical applications of electricity. His three most important successes were his creation of a comprehensive electricity grid for Bavaria, thus, the state became Germany's 'first territorial state to have a statewide electricity provision'; the Walchenseewerk, still home to one of Germany's largest power stations; and for coming up with the idea and pushing through his concept for the Deutsches Museum.

In 1906, the first Deutsches Museum was opened in the former Bavarian National Museum (now the Museum of Ethnology) while today's museum was in the process of being constructed (and did not finally open until 7 May 1925 due to the outbreak of the First World War and Germany's economic problems after 1918). According to Heckl, the very raison d'être behind Miller creating the museum has hardly changed: 'The idea [was to have] a huge place where not only masterpieces [of science and technology] are displayed behind glass, but somewhere to engage people in discussion forums and also engage them in haptic experiences.' Though it is entitled a 'German' museum as opposed to a

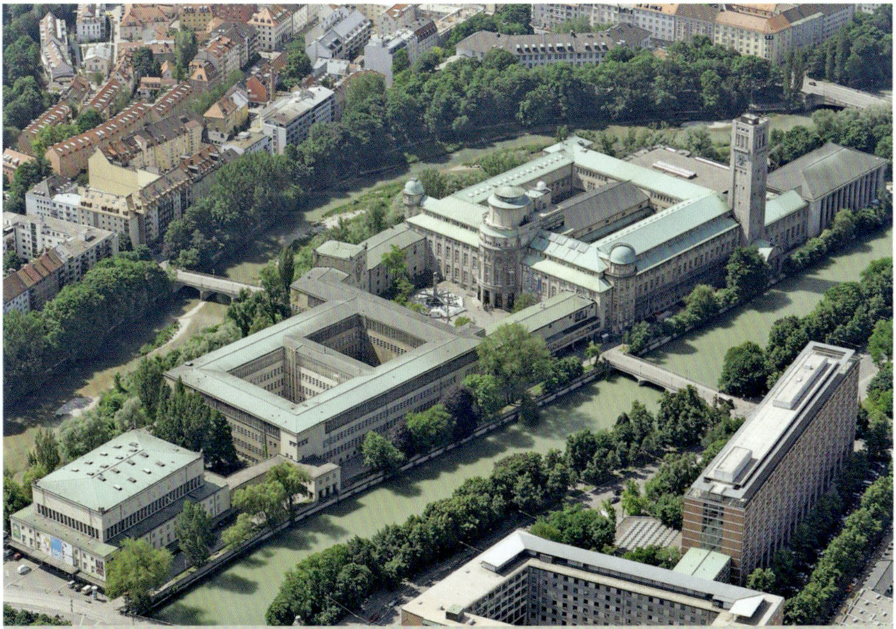

Professor Wolfgang Heckl, director of the Deutsches Museum (above)

On the Deustches Museum

Oskar von Miller said that displaying the artefacts of science and technology is not only to educate people about 'great Germans' and 'Nobel Prize winners', and inventions and discoveries, but to discuss with people the complicated – even more today – way to the future ... No political decision can be made these days without a strong basis in natural science and technology. Think about a genome sequence or an ageing society ... The future of science depends on inventions and discoveries; but 99 per cent of the population are not experts, and the idea is to bring them together in the forum of the Deutsches Museum. It's a 'public outreach centre', in modern words.

On the history of the museum

You know there are 10,000 professors in Germany. There is only one job following Oskar von Miller. My grandfather and my grandmother were here in 1906, and these are the oldest entrance cards we have in the Deutsches Museum. I found them in the boxes I got from the house of my grandmother. Even in the museum archive we don't have such cards any more ... They are a piece of the history of the Deutsches Museum.

On his own research
My scientific results are on display at the Deutsches Museum. I was the first person to get real images of DNA molecules with a microscope. And now I have my own students doing work in the museum … The Open Science Lab [is] a new concept at museums: people not only see the end process of technology, the Nobel Prize winners and so on, but they see how science is made. My PhD students work in the open, in the laboratory, in the Deutsches Museum. Visitors come and ask questions: What are you doing here? What are you spending tax-payers money on?

'Munich' or 'Bavarian' one, to a degree, since the late 1950s, the museum represents not only how Bavarian policy makers have come to perceive their capital city, but also how they have attempted to showcase Munich as the pinnacle of post-war German economic modernisation. To be absolutely clear, there is often a degree of hyperbole involved in the promotion of the city as a high-tech destination. But as will be shown below, the economic success of Munich in the past 50 years owes a massive debt to its ability to attract some of Europe's best scientific brains and most innovative companies.

The museum works closely with the Fraunhofer-Gesellschaft, the Max Planck Institut, the Ludwig-Maximilians-Universität and the Technische Universität München, as well as the Martinsried and Garching research clusters, all of which have been instrumental in raising Munich to become arguably Germany's premier high-tech location. Building on the traditions of scientific exploration in the manner of Fraunhofer, Pettenkofer and Linde, the Deutsches Museum is an integral part of the promotion of Munich as a city that treasures its past while embracing the future. It hardly seemed likely in 1945.

From Destruction to the Home of High Technology

The instability across the Weimar Republic of the post-First World War years, encompassing defeat, revolution, hyperinflation and a lack of regime legitimacy, was, as shown earlier, exacerbated in Munich by the radical right-wing response to the short-lived Räterepublik of 1919. In the latter half of the 1920s, the economic and political situation appeared to have settled somewhat, but the 1929 Wall Street Crash engendered devastating political and socio-economic circumstances never before seen in one country on such a scale. It was this that facilitated the rise of the Nazi movement into a mass party and opened the door to its subsequent takeover of power in Germany.

Munich emerged from the ruins of the Second World War seemingly broken in every possible respect, from the political to the moral to the economic. Though the rebuilding of the German economy can be said to have started with the all-important currency reform of 1948, things really took off for Munich in the late 1950s and early 1960s, coinciding with – but distinct in some ways from – the wider West German *Wirtschaftswunder*, which saw rapid economic recovery fuelled by startling growth rates and productivity levels. The result was two-fold: Munich was transformed from the capital of the most underdeveloped of all West German states to the dynamic capital of a Bavaria that today can lay claim to be not only the most technologically advanced state in Germany, but one of the most innovative regions in the European Union.

Much of the credit for this has been laid at the feet of Franz Josef Strauß (1915-1988), the charismatic CSU politician, a man who divided opinion with apparent ease and who was – and more than 20 years after his death still is – popular and unpopular in equal measure. Accusations of corruption do not seem to have done his reputation across Bavaria much harm, and CSU politicians very quickly get tetchy if his almost saintly image is questioned. The degree of influence Strauß had on the economic rise of Bavaria is hotly contested, but there is little doubt that he played a vital role in enticing important firms and research institutes to relocate from northern Germany south to Bavaria, invariably to Munich.

Munich did have something of a provenance as a city of innovation; but even with the likes of Joseph von Fraunhofer, Max von Pettenkofer, Carl von Linde and Oskar von Miller, Munich had never been seen as a centre of innovation on any sizeable scale, and prior to 1945 technically advanced firms and institutes were much more likely to be located in the north, most notably Dahlem, Berlin. But with the former capital firmly located in East Germany, opportunities opened up for western locations to establish themselves as leading centres of research.

When, in 1949, the newly created Fraunhofer-Gesellschaft was established in Munich under the patronage of CSU politician Hanns Seidel (1901-1961), with a remit to be national in its scope, it failed to garner much support from its home state and received a miserly subvention of 1,000 German marks. It

Franz Josef Strauss, Bavarian Minister President, hands Margaret Thatcher, British Prime Minister, a porcelain Bavarian lion (23 March 1979)

was a similar story for the great German scientist Werner Heisenberg's (1901-1976) wish to relocate his Max Planck Institute for Physics to Munich. It was primarily through the perseverance of Strauß in 1955, in his role as West Germany's minister of atomic affairs, that the institute finally settled in the city, along with the country's first atomic reactor. Indeed, in the 1950s, Strauß also took it upon himself to wield his considerable influence to save Audi and BMW, at that time two virtually bankrupt firms, but today two of Bavaria's most renowned brands. In addition, the early 1960s saw a network of Max Planck institutes sprout up across Germany, the most important located in Munich. In retrospect, it is clear that Munich was reaching something of a turning point in its economic development. As Mark Milosch has shown, the Munich Research Reactor had enabled the physics department of Munich's Technical University to become a centre of atomic sciences, while Garching, formely little more than a village on the northern edge of the city, began to emerge as the 'German Oxford' with its research into atomic fusion. In the process, some kind of critical mass was reached as more and more research institutes migrated to, or were established in, Garching.

To a degree, Munich had an inbuilt advantage over many of its German competitors in that it never had to expend too much energy on transforming once dynamic but by the 1970s 'burdensome' heavy industrial areas. By the same time, Garching had become established as a world-class centre of scientific research, boasting some of the leading lights in, for example, plasmaphysics, radiochemistry and low-temperature research. In other Munich locations, centres for radiology were established and a Siemens centre focusing on reactor development was created at huge expense. Further research institutes related to flight technologies were set up at the Oberpfaffenhofen airfield, east of Munich, leading to German aerospace research being concentrated in and around the Munich area. From his position as German defence minister, Strauß had done his best to ensure that Munich became the undisputed centre of high-tech aerospace research.

Of course, it would be remiss to paint a one-dimensional picture: other areas of Germany have also established oustanding research institutes, for example around the Rhine area and in Heidelberg. And in biotechnology, for example, Munich, though one of the best in Europe, cannot be considered the equal of a Cambridge (UK), for instance. Similarly, it would be wholly inaccurate to give the impression that Munich was somehow immune to the ravages of economic cycles or the effects of world economic downturns: the city was hit by Germany's first major post-war recession of 1966/67, the stagflation of the 1970s, the boom and then recession in the wake of German reunification that blighted the German economy in the 1990s and the most recent downturn in the world economy from 2008. Overall, however, the story has been one of remarkable success and the Greater Munich Area is the centre of high-tech industry in Bavaria, itself a leading economic region in Europe's biggest economy, Germany.

Population

It is difficult to conceive of Munich as a 'global city' in the manner of London or New York or even Berlin and its population is certainly not as profoundly diverse. With people from around 180 countries, however, it is a genuinely multi-ethnic city. From 1955, migrant workers from principally Yugoslavia,

Italy, Spain, Greece, Portugal and Turkey were actively recruited to Germany in order to continue the post-war rebuilding and then the modernisation of its cities and infrastructure. In 1973 it was decided that these approximately four million workers and families who had made a huge contribution to Germany's post-war *Wirtschaftswunder*, and who had made West Germany their home, were no longer wanted and were refused citizenship under the official notion that 'Germany is not a country of immigration'. As Simon Green has pointed out, this means that there is the extraordinary scenario of 'a third generation of "foreigners" (in legal terms only) growing up in Germany today.' Paradoxically, since 1945 Germany has taken in more refugees and asylum seekers than any other European country.

By the end of 2003, 7.3 million non-German nationals were living in the country, comprising 8.9 per cent of the total population. Of the 1.37 million inhabitants of Munich in 2007, 311,321 were foreign. Of these foreigners, the highest numbers from the European Union were: Greece, Italy and Austria at more than 21,000 each, followed by 15,118 from Poland. Less well represented, though still substantial, were 7,403 from France, 5,330 from Romania and just under 5,000 from both the United Kingdom and from Hungary. In addition, a sizeable minority originate from the former Yugoslavia: 16,502 from Bosnia-Herzegovina, 24,646 from Croatia, 13,387 from Serbia and 151 from Montenegro. Outside Europe, 10,353 were from the continent of Africa, 5,570 from the USA, 4,217 from Afghanistan and 8,139 from Iraq. The largest non-German population in Munich in 2007, however, was the 42,662 from Turkey, many of whom, in the words of Simon Green, are 'foreigners' in 'legal terms only'.

Economic Strengths

The 1990 reunification of Germany in the wake of the fall of communism in eastern Europe led to the much-disputed 1999 relocation of the country's capital from Bonn to Berlin. Munich's claim to be Germany's 'secret capital' now had little – not even ironic – resonance and there was the justified fear that the economic and political influence Munich had painstakingly garnered over the previous five decades was imperilled. Indeed, just as much (not all) of the apparatus of national government moved from Bonn to Berlin, so a few businesses and institutions decided that it would be in their interests to relocate their headquarters from Munich to the new capital, producing a slightly hysterical reaction from some quarters in Munich. In truth, Munich has remained one of the prime locations for German and international companies to invest in, and a reunified Berlin has done little to change that. Part of the reason for the economic success of the city is the so-called 'Münchner Mix', which refers to the healthy combination of industrial sectors and the city's mix of global companies and small and medium-sized enterprises (SMEs).

The work done in the 1950s and 1960s, therefore, continues to pay off and the Greater Munich Area is the centre of high-tech clusters and is home to around 25 world-class research institutions. The 13 Munich Max Planck institutes (plus the general administration), for example, employ around 3,750 people, most prominently in the natural and life sciences, while the Fraunhofer-Gesellschaft has five institutes in Munich, focusing on high-tech engineering. Of Bavaria's 19 official 'clusters', the Greater Munich Area has clusters in media, information and communication technology (ICT), financial services, biotechnology, nanotechnology, the automobile sector, air and aerospace, satellite navigation, environmental technology and medicine.

The Großhadern-Martinsried biotechnology cluster, for example, makes a substantial contribution to Munich's reputation as a European leader in the field. Garching has four Max Planck institutes, the European Southern Observatory and various departments from the Technische Universität München (TUM) and the Ludwig-Maximilians-Universität München (LMU). It was further strengthened in 2004 by the addition of a new research reactor and by the opening in the same year of the US giant General Electric's European research centre.

Ahead of Berlin and Hamburg, Munich has more software companies than anywhere else in Germany, contributing more than 10 billion euros to the national economy and in 2003 employing more than 54,000 people. Around 14,000 people work in the production of medicine in the Munich area, more than 9,000 in environment technology and by the middle of 2000 in Europe only London and Paris employed more people in the booming information and communication technology industry. The city is second to Frankfurt as Germany's banking centre and is home to Allianz, the world's biggest insurance firm, plus Münchner Rück, the world's largest reinsurance company, both contributing to Munich's reputation as the insurance and reinsurance capital of Germany.

The impact of the huge world economic downturn from 2008 has clearly had an effect and it will be interesting to note how this hits Munich's insurance and other branches in the long term. In addition, in the past four or five years the city's IT industry appears to have been adversely affected by a slowdown, resulting in fewer workplaces.

With a profusion of research institutes and leading firms, it is no surprise that Upper Bavaria, led by its capital, Munich, is one of the few European regions to surpass the European Union's aim of investing 3 per cent of GDP annually in R&D (research and development). Upper Bavaria's 4.6 per cent spending on R&D in 2003 places it fifth in the EU league table, while Leo van den Berg has estimated that more than 50,000 people worked in the sector in 2005. This attention to R&D is reflected in the prestige attached to Munich's TUM and LMU, both ranked among Germany's best five universities (some studies suggest the best two, though they still lag some way behind the best in the UK and even further behind the best in the US), while both have close ties to Munich research institutes and businesses. This focus on R&D is backed by figures showing that Munich vies with Stuttgart as Germany's most active patent area (2,474 for 2007), supported by the location of the German Patent Office and the European Patent Office in the city.

Munich also has Germany's lowest big-city unemployment figures: according to the Bundesagentur für Arbeit (Germany's state employment agency), the city had an unemployment rate in November 2008 of 4.1 per cent, which by November 2009 had risen to around 4.9 per cent, still low compared with the Germany average of more than 7.1 per cent for November 2008 and 7.6 for November 2009. For the same periods, Stuttgart recorded unemployment figures of 4.5 per cent (2008) and 5.6 per cent (2009), while figures for Frankfurt were 6.2 per cent and 6.3 per cent, Hamburg 7.7 per cent and 8.4 per cent and Berlin a desperate 12.7 per cent and 13.3 per cent.

Munich is the centre of Germany's media industry and between 1999 and 2002 the number of media firms in the Greater Munich Area grew from 11,425 to more than 14,000. At the same time, the number of workers in the sector climbed from 116,000 to a huge 187,000 and turnover from 19.2 billion euros to 24.5 billion euros. Munich has around ten radio stations and is home to numerous national television companies, both branches employing a total of around 4,000 people. As the centre of the German film industry, the

Munich area is home to many film and film production companies and other ancillary firms, most famously Bavaria Film, a film and production company in Geiselgasteig, in Munich's Grünwald suburb. It was there in 1925 that British filmmaker Alfred Hitchcock made his first film, *The Pleasure Garden*; other film luminaries to ply their trade at Bavaria Film at one time or another were Ingmar Bergman, Stanley Kubrick, Billy Wilder, Rainer Werner Fassbinder and Wolfgang Petersen. With around 250 publishing houses (including major names such as C.H. Beck, Langenscheidt, Deutscher Taschenbuch Verlag, Piper and art specialists such as Prestel, Hirmer and Bruckmann, as well as various houses focusing on Munich and Bavarian history and culture) and around 11,000 titles produced yearly, not only has Munich by far the largest number of publishers in Germany, but only New York in the world has more.

Munich is home to four principal daily newspapers, including Germany's biggest-selling quality daily, the *Süddeutsche Zeitung* (*SZ*), which sells an average of 445,000 a day across Germany. The *Frankfurter Allgemeiner Zeitung* (*FAZ*), the *Süddeutsche*'s nearest rival, lags around 80,000 copies behind on 366,478, with *Die Welt* trailing further on 271,370. In addition to the *SZ*, there is the serious-minded and somewhat conservative *Münchner Merkur*, as well as the *Abendzeitung* (*AZ*) and *Tageszeitung* (*TZ*), both tabloids.

With 93 km of U-Bahn (underground) lines, 442 km of S-Bahn (suburban railway) lines, and 71 km of tram lines, the expanding Munich public transport system is among the best and most reliable in Europe, although to the irritation of the population, it is not without delays and breakdowns, primarily due to greater demand, meaning increasing numbers of trains in decreasing time frames.

The occasional late train, however, does not prevent Munich from being named in a host of surveys as the city in which most Germans would prefer to live. Similarly, people do not seem to be put off by the fact that in 2007, at 260 euros per square metre a month (as reported in the *Süddeutsche Zeitung*), Munich's Kaufingerstraße was named as Germany's most expensive street in which to rent retail space. Frankfurt's main shopping street, by comparison, came in at 225 euros per square metre, though neither could compete with New York's astronomical 999 euros per square metre. In a similar study by Cushman & Wakefield in 2009, it was calculated monthly retail rents in New York had risen to more than 1000 and in Munich to 300 euros per square metre a month respectively. Nor are people discouraged by the fact that nu-

Some undergound stations, such as Candidplatz above, have been praised for their imaginative designs.

merous cost-of-living surveys consistently name Munich as Germany's most expensive city (athough in 2008 consulting firm Mercer placed Munich some way down the world list in 37th place).

According to Leo van den Berg's comparative study of *European Cities in the Knowledge Economy*, 'Munich's quality of life has been a key driver of its economic success'. It is not surprising to learn, therefore, that Münchners are regularly calculated as having the highest standard of living in Germany and in the top ten in Europe.

Munich, however, is far from the nirvana that statisticians, business leaders and city promoters can sometimes appear to portray. Little is heard from such people about the sometimes visceral opposition from some in the city to the building of a much-needed new mosque for the city's Muslim population. Furthermore, in contrast to the city's bohemian past, and compared with Berlin, London or Amsterdam, for example, the city has little of what is termed 'underground' or 'alternative' cultures, which are so integral to the creativity of young people in the arts and music. This has been cited as a motivating fac-

By the end of the 1950s, Munich's Karlsplatz was the busiest traffic point in Europe

tor for some to leave Munich for the more amenable and less 'stuffy' Berlin or Hamburg. In contrast, Van den Berg also points out that 'Munich has no clear spatial concentrations of social and economic problems, or "problem neighbourhoods,"' and the city tends not to have the very deep social problems that afflict many other cities. But while the average income of German citizens in Munich in 2005 was 1,710 euros per month, it was just 1,010 euros for non-Germans, a difference of 40 per cent and growing. Therefore, inequality is rising in Munich, as it is across Germany, though it is still some way behind the United States and Great Britain. In addition, even with its very good public transport system, the city is often congested, while returning to the city from a weekend trip to the Alps by car frequently entails sitting in traffic jams. More importantly, the lack of affordable housing is a perennial problem, a particular gripe of old Münchners, who are also often heard bemoaning the disappearance of the Bavarian accent from Munich's streets as more 'foreigners', meaning non-Bavarians, move in and locals move out, something that has certainly made Munich a less distinctive *Bavarian* city than it was 40 years ago.

The lack of affordable housing has created a problem for the city's two principal universities, the LMU and TMU, and though progress has been made in this regard, some critics have indicated that if the city wants to dissuade the best students (Munich has around 80,000 university students) from opting for what are deemed more 'youth-friendly cities', particularly Berlin, much more needs to done.

Economically, Munich had an exceptional 2007, but by 2009 city officials were keen to point out that tax revenue from business could be reduced by as much as a third by 2010, down from 1.9 billion euros to 1.3 billion euros. In addition, a July 2009 report commissioned by the German magazine *Capital* claimed that of all Germany cities, Hamburg is currently best positioned to deal with the prevailing economic difficulties up until 2015. Though Munich did come out in second place, that it was not first was seen in some quarters as significant. In another of these currently ubiquitous reports, the Institute of German Economics surprisingly reported that 'southern Germany has been hit harder by the current recession than the country's north and east' (admittedly from a lower base), with the significant caveat that 'only the Munich metropolitan area has managed to escape the worst of the recession'.

While it is still too early to make sweeping economic predictions, the available evidence strongly suggests that Munich will maintain its position as one of Europe's best performing economies. In short, this represents nothing short of an astounding transformation. What was in the early 1950s the capital of a provincial and predominantly agricultural state, a city with more hang-ups about Berlin than seems natural, Munich is now the axis of a Bavaria that is recognised across Germany as the pre-eminent high-tech centre of the country. And nowhere has the transformation been greater than in the capital itself. Initially not by grand design, and without any real overall visionary plan, Munich became home to research centres, innovative, forward-thinking firms and a host of entrepreneurs. There was a degree of provenance to this transformation with Fraunhofer, Pettenkofer, followed by Linde and Miller, all four innovators in different ways. But the scale of change in the wake of the war-time devastation of the city's infrastructure, housing and economy is monumental. A city that had always wanted to be measured by its contribution to high culture, particularly in art, architecture and stage, succeeded in an even bigger way though its industry and economy.

Chapter 6

ART, ARCHITECTURE & PLACE

~

Clichés & Tourism

An analysis entitled 'Regional Ranking 2009' by the Institut der deutschen Wirtschaft Köln, which uses indicators such as standard of living, the labour market, infrastructure and location, placed the Greater Munich Area ahead of any other area in Germany. Along with the city itself, 'six of its surrounding areas' are placed in 'the best 11 cities and districts' in Germany. Overall, the core city itself came out on top; neighbouring Starnberg came second. Similarly, in a wide-ranging survey based on criteria ranging from economic factors to health and public services, consulting firm Mercer rated Munich as seventh in the world in its 2008 list of 'top cities offering the best quality of life'.

On the one hand, few of these surveys bother sullying this image with Munich's – according to critics – at times frustrating innate conservatism, which is said to affect everything from its architecture to its long-standing inability to come to terms with its Nazi past. On the other hand, even with the necessary caveat that a large degree of healthy scepticism should be applied, it is indicative of the high regard in which the city is held that Munich comes out consistently well in survey after survey, in report after report, year after year. As the city's press department enjoys pointing out, even respected international newspapers have recently joined in the praise, for example when on 13 April 2008 *The New York Times* ran a report headlined 'Munich Reduxed: Germany's Hot Spot of the Moment'. Likewise, a year earlier, *Monocle* magazine's yearly review named Munich the 'most liveable city in the world' (subsequently dropping it to second place in 2008, then to fourth in 2009).

Nevertheless, Munich still tends to engender its fair share of stereotyping and over-generalisations. Respected travel guide *The Lonely Planet* (online version) has described the city thus:

> Pulsing with prosperity and *Gemütlichkeit* (cosiness), Munich (München) revels in its own contradictions. Folklore and age-old traditions exist side by side with sleek BMWs, designer boutiques and high-powered industry. Its museums include world-class collections of artistic masterpieces, and its music and cultural scenes give Berlin a run for its money. Despite all its sophistication, Munich retains a touch of provincialism that visitors find charming. The people's attitude is one of live and let live – and Müncheners will be the first to admit that their 'metropolis' is little more than a *Weltdorf*, a world village. During Oktoberfest representatives of the entire planet turn out to toast the town.

The usual Munich clichés of '*Gemütlichkeit*', 'live and let live' and '*Weltdorf*' are all there, but it is the more perceptive elements that are most revealing: 'Pulsating with prosperity', 'sleek BMWs, designer boutiques and high-powered industry' and 'world-class collections of artistic masterpieces, and its music and cultural scenes give Berlin a run for its money'.

Regarding numbers of visitors to the city, Munich had 4.7 million 'guests' in 2007, putting the city below the very highest echelons of the most visited cities in Europe. The highest number of visitors from abroad come from the USA (2007: 304,197; 2008: 264,196), Italy (237,686; 237,924), United Kingdom and Northern Ireland (195,113; 188,089), Switzerland (147,213; 152,954) and Austria (125,359; 131,376).

Munich is never going to rival London, Paris and New York for sheer visitor numbers; its medium size and population of just 1.37 million puts it in an altogether different league. The salient point about Munich's high number of visitors, however, is that compared with many other European cities that attract major tourist numbers, Munich is neither a capital city nor what could be described as a 'global city'. There are many reasons why Munich is such a hot spot for visitors: as seen in earlier chapters, the city's long and rarely dull history; its elevated reputation as a city of culture and of high-tech business; and its prime location, geographically in central Europe, an hour or so from the Alps, with warm summers and snowy winters. Furthermore, while 'brand Munich' is exceptionally successful in its own right, it receives more attention than most on account of being home to one of the world's most high-profile football clubs in Bayern Munich.

Churches & the Battle for the Skyline

It is probably with some relief that contemporary Munich economists, politicians and business leaders recall the decision to recreate much of Munich's Altstadt in the wake of the destruction of the Second World War. It is unlikely that millions of visitors would descend on the city centre to see grey concrete buildings, paradoxically, in the manner of the much-disliked Kaufhaus department store at one corner of the historic Marienplatz.

With the rebuild, Munich's 16th- and 17th-century history as a centre of strict religious observance – most importantly as a centre of the counter-Reformation – is clearly discernible. St Peter's is the city centre's oldest parish church, originally built in 1181 (in fact, excavations in 1952/53 revealed the foundations of an earlier brick basilica, though the first known mention of a church was in a 1225 document), more than 20 years after Munich's foundation, and greatly extended during the next 50 years. In the great fire of 1327, which destroyed a third of the city, with the exception of its western part most of St Peter's was reduced to little more than ashes. The rebuilding started in 1329 and the church was consecrated in 1368. Over the following three centuries, St Peter's was extended and altered in a variety of ways, though maintaining much of its gothic appearance. It was given a partial internal and external baroque renovation in the 17th century, most notably the replacement of the gothic choir by a grander baroque interpretation, plus new altars, an organ gallery and new side entrances. With the exception of the removal of its cemetery in 1777, the external appearance of the church, in essence, did not alter until it was almost completely destroyed by Allied bombs during the Second World War, after which, it was rebuilt. The interior underwent another makeover during the 18th century, which included works of art by Johann Baptist Straub and Ignaz Günther (1725-1775), both reflecting the rococo style of the age, while the church won the addition of an Austrian cannonball – apparently having missed its intended target of Revolutionary French troops – which is said to be still firmly embedded in the church's brickwork.

There is little doubt that many Münchners recognise the importance of St Peter's to the history of the city. But, in truth, it stands in the shadow of the impossibly domineering Frauenkirche, which more than any other building in Munich is the undisputed symbol of the city. When built, ostensibly between

St Peter's, the oldest church in Munich's Altstadt

1468 and 1488, the Frauenkirche – or to be more precise, Dom zu Unserer lieben Frau – became Munich's second parish church, St Peter's being the first. The Frauenkirche was, in fact, not the first church built at its location. An older version, a Marienkirche, covering around two-thirds the size of its huge successor, was erected by the ruling Wittelsbachs in around 1240 (purportedly, records from the latter half of the 12th century show an even earlier Roman 'Marienkapelle' or 'Chapel of Our Lady' in the vicinity), featuring a vaulted structure and, unusually for the period, three naves, plus twin towers. Accompanied by Johann Tulbeck (d. 1476), the Bishop of Freising and a host of other dignitaries, Duke Sigmund laid the foundation stone of the Frauenkirche on 9 February 1468. Master builder Jörg von Halspach's monumental late-Gothic church, with its enormous hall, constructed predominantly of red brick, was possibly influenced by the Dome of the Rock in Jerusalem, which at the time was widely available as a woodcut and which Halspach presumably saw. According to some sources, wood for the roof alone required up to 1400 barges in order to transport it along the river Isar to the building site. Fantastically, it took just 20 years for the whole gigantic construction task to be completed (a record for a building of such scale), save the characteristic 'onion dome' cupolas, added in around 1525. In the year of its completion, 1488, its designer, Jörg von Halspach, died, making him one of a very few people to take on and – just about – witness the completion of such a monumen-

Renate Schostack, former Munich-based cultural correspondent for the ***Frankfurter Allgemeiner Zeitung***, wrote a heartfelt account of Munich. Often critical but not without warm admiration, she called her book *Die eitle Schöne* (*The Vain Beauty*)

On her first visit to Munich

Munich was in part still in ruins in 1958 … The opera house was still in ruins: part of Maximilianstraße, part of Sendlingerstraße, only one storey, shops and nothing else. There were still tramways through the middle of the city, through Marienplatz, no pedestrian zone, that came much later. People were very differently dressed, very formal. One said, of course, '*Fräulein*' and '*Herr*'. Also, people were dressed in a bourgeois way, very polite. In a way it was nice, but the atmosphere was also stiff. One didn't talk about the war, about Hitler. In 1958 there was also the 800-year [city foundation] celebrations and that was a great thing for Munich at the time because it was like an absolution … [from] Hitler. Because many envoys from other university towns around Europe came, with the provost of Edinburgh, who looked the best because he had a very good gown. They walked through Munich in a procession and it was a great thing. They went to the Deutsches Museum and Werner Heisenberg held a great speech there.

Compared with other cities

In my book I quoted Sir Peter Jones [the British director of the Bavarian State Opera between 1993 and 2006]: 'We are a small city but we have great culture,' which is true. Munich has one of the opera houses with the best reputations in the world. In a league with La Scala, the Metropolitan and the London [Royal] Opera House. The theatres in Munich are amongst the best in Germany, and at times they were the best … The museums are marvellous, though not as big as the National [Gallery] in London and the Victoria & Albert, but they have the very top works of art. Smaller in quantity, but not in quality … The theatre in Berlin is, I think, not as good as in Munich. They have a good opera house, they can compete, I think. And they have very good museums, because they were assembled by the Prussian rulers through centuries … For young people and for working artists, it seems to be more interesting to be there. It's a much bigger city … but I don't think it's a competitor to Munich. I think it's something different.

On Catholicism in the city

Go on a Sunday to the city's churches. They are all full. But it is a cultural event, and they have wonderful music and you don't have to pay. If you have no money for concerts then go to the city churches. They have wonderful choirs and orchestras, and so on, all different.

tal construction. In line with the practice of the period, though increasingly controversial, the Pope authorised the sale of indulgences to help finance the Frauenkirche, prompting around 123,000 pilgrims to stream through Munich between 1480 and 1482.

As with St Peter's, the Frauenkirche has been furnished in various styles through the centuries, notably gaining a late-Renaissance/early baroque interior between 1601 and 1622, which included a new monumental high altar in 1620. In the 1770s, the Frauenkirche lost its stained-glass windows, received a gothic makeover in the mid-1800s, including the removal of the now unfashionable baroque elements, followed by the re-placement of the stained-glass windows, before the church was restored to its original colour between 1930-1932. Just as with St Peter's, the Frauenkirche was hugely damaged during Allied air raids in the last years of the Second World War, before eventually being restored in three main phases to its present regal state.

More than 400 years after it was first built, the Frauenkirche still counts as one of the largest halled-churches in southern Germany, measuring 108 metres long, 38 metres wide and with its two towers just short of 100 metres in height. This 'short of 100 metres' is significant, much to the consternation of some modern Munich architects and the ruling mayor, Christian Ude, of the SPD. In a 2004 citizen-petition, headed by ex-mayor of Munich Georg Kronawitter (also SPD), a narrow majority of 50.4 per cent (on a miserly turnout of just 21.9 per cent) of Munich residents rejected the construction of any building higher than the magical figure of 99 metres within the confines of the city's Mittlere Ring, the city's middle of three ring roads. Though only binding for a year, this attempt to prevent – as some saw it – a possible blighting of the architecture and charm of Munich's Altstadt means that no high buildings are likely to built any time soon in the vicinity of the Frauenkirche. To critics, this merely confirmed Munich's reputation as a city of 'conservatism'. While the

Built in the 1920s, the Technical Rathaus was one of Germany's first high-rise building

reputation is not entirely undeserved, this does not mean that Munich lacks modern architecture: many 'tall' buildings had already been built prior to the 2004 vote; more importantly, buildings do not have to be 'tall' to be architecturally innovative.

An example is the Technisches Rathaus and adjoining gas works (Technical Town Hall), located on Blumenstraße, on the edge of the Altstadt. Built in the 1920s, it was recently described by Leif Jerram in *Germany's Other Modernity* as arguably meant to project a sense of a Munich relaxed with architectural modernism, this, paradoxically, at a time when Munich was becoming a haven of reaction and extremism. Reflecting the takeover of city planning from royal and religious authorities to a more government-bureaucratic axis over the previous 50 years, Jerram notes that 'the Technical Rathaus complex represented a bold and committed statement of engagement with modernity at the heart of the old city.'

Designed by Hermann Leitensdorfer, the construction – or its most recognisable section – became Germany's first modern *Hochhaus*, or 'high-rise'. Although at the time the *Münchner Neueste Nachrichten* praised the building as having 'something of the old Munich spiritual quest without the olde worlde touches', Jerram shows that with a few exceptions the design was widely criticised. Publications as diverse as the NSDAP organ the *Völkischer Beobachter*, which labelled it 'a giant barracks with six floors', and the *Allgemeine Zeitung*, which described it as 'boring, factory-like, devoted to over-functionalism', led the way. Within a few years, however, the building got a more sympathetic hearing from press and public alike, so much so that Jerram describes the Munich population as having a 'near-Damascene conversion' in favour of the building. Today, renamed Städtisches Planungshochhaus, the 45-metre-high

building serves as an impressive though rather ignored location for a section of Munich's city planning authority.

Though Munich does not have modern skyscrapers comparable size-wise to Shanghai and New York or even Frankfurt and London, there are a handful of architecturally innovative high-rise buildings in the city. Most notable of these are the 146-metre-high Uptown Munich (completed in 2005) on Georg-Brauchle-Ring, while the 84-metre-high Skyline Tower on the corner of Walter-Gropius-Straße should be competed in early 2010 at a cost of around 200 million euros. Perhaps most impressive is the rather unimpressively named Highlight Munich Business Towers, consisting of two interconnected structures, one 113 metres high, the other measuring 123 metres. Clearly visible to visitors heading south to the city from the airport, the elegant, slim and predominantly glass towers contain – as the name suggests – numerous offices, as well as a four-star hotel.

Although there is an element of caricature to the way critics portray Munich, there is undoubtedly a prevailing 'conservatism' about many aspects of the city, from politics to art and from history to architecture. In truth, and for better or worse, since before the Second World War, Munich has, arguably, only fleetingly been at the avant-garde end of construction projects. Perhaps, the two most notable of the large-scale post-war architectural innovations were a corollary to the city being awarded the 1972 Olympics and to Germany winning the race to host the 2006 football World Cup (more of which is covered in chapter seven). Current plans include a new Hauptbahnhof (main train station). The city's first station was built in 1839, though it did not last a decade as the wooden construction burned down in 1847, and it was followed in 1849 by a new so-called Centralbahnhof. At 111 metres long, 20 metres wide with barrel-vaulted ceilings and arched arcades, it was likened to a church, hence its moniker of the 'Basilica of Traffic'. Germany's rapid industrialisation in the wake of unification in 1871 meant that transport infrastructure was quickly modernised around the country, and Munich's main station (again called Hauptbahnhof) was expanded to cope with the extra demands, notably 1857-1860, 1876-1880, in 1893 and 1921, in the process becoming the first station in the country to receive electric lighting.

Left: the face of modern Munich? A number of Münchners were unhappy about the location of the Highlight Munich Business Towers

BMW Welt and the BMW Museum (behind, right)

Since before the Second World War there have been periodic plans to transfer Munich's main station to a more suitable location, away from the inner city (a new main station was also a central aspect of the grandiose plans for Hitler's 'new Munich' in the 1930s). Still periodically discussed, it would seem that the city's infrastructure developments are now far too developed and entwined for this to become a reality. The last realistic opportunity was in the wake of the destruction of the inner city in 1945, which included much of the main station. Current plans are for a radical and futuristic remodification of the existing station, the competition for which was won by architects Auer & Weber, though the estimated 350-million-euro cost of the project soon meant the plans ran into difficulties. A modified plan, including an already started second commuter (S-Bahn) line, has given hope the whole project could be completed by 2018.

If realised, the new main station would join a handful of other futuristic designs that could go some way to altering the city's conservative image to – if not quite avant-garde – perhaps a city that is more prepared to take risks. For some observers, this has already started, notably the new BMW Welt building, with its 'whirlwind' front façade, and its wave-like roof that was specifically designed to complement the nearby Olympic complex. Other recent examples are a handful of innovative underground station constructions (including an art gallery, others with imaginative interior designs), the Fünf Höfe (an impressively lit shopping and gastronomy passage, plus art gallery, the whole concept from fêted architecture firm Herzog & de Meuron), a host of indoor and outdoor swimming pools, one of Europe's best airports as well as a first-rate trade-fair complex (at the former airport at Riem) and superb, modern museum architecture. Still, it is 'old Munich' – Marienplatz, the towering though rather plain Frauenkirche and the far more elaborate interiors and exteriors of a whole host of churches – that attracts many tourists.

While the Frauenkirche, therefore, is set to keep its role as the most instantly recognisable building in the city centre, the Jesuit church St Michael's, located between Marienplatz and Karlsplatz, played a much more important role in the city's history in the late 16th century and well into the 17th century. Famously, it was Duke Albrecht V who in 1559 brought the Jesuits to Munich in order to do battle on the home front against the teachings of Martin Luther. And as religious lines hardened across Europe, intensifying the battle between Reformation and Counter-Reformation, Munich became a central axis of anti-Protestantism. In 1583, Bavaria's Duke Wilhelm V laid the cornerstone for the extensive Jesuit school and adjoining St Michael's church in his capital. Completed in 1597, St Michael's is the largest Renaissance church in northern Europe, and, after St Peter's in Rome, it has the second largest barrel vault in the world. Furthermore, it provided a model for church architecture in

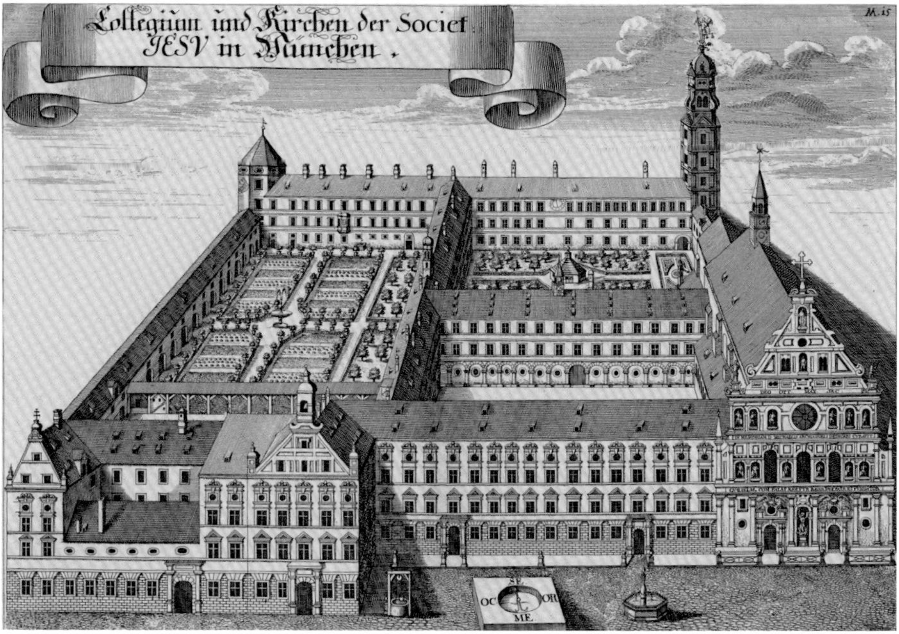

St Michael's and the vast Jesuit complex (etching by Michael Wening from around 1700)

southern Germany for the following two centuries, representing a triumphal symbol of Counter-Reformation architecture.

Much more of an issue for the Munich population, however, was the impact the ultra strict Jesuits had on pressuring the population into strict adherence to Catholic worship, meaning everything from regular church attendance to observance of religious festivals. Moreover, generations of royalty and members of Munich's patrician class grew up schooled by pious Jesuit scholars, influencing the city not just with regard to religion, but also culturally, particularly in terms of music, singing and art. In the 17th century, opera was heavily propagandised, most patently when used by Jesuit scholars to impart a moral message to the seemingly 'never-pious-enough' general populace. Similarly, classical mythology was used in stage plays to pay obsequious homage to whomever happened to be on the Bavarian throne at the time. The battle of religions was won, at least in Munich, by Catholicism, and the city remained a Catholic stronghold until well into the twentieth century, though contemporary figures suggest this is diminishing: in 2007 the city's 1.35 million population was 38.9 per cent Catholic, 14.1 per cent Protestant, 0.3 per cent 'Israeli' (the city's description) and 46.6 per cent 'other'.

The Jesuit stranglehold on religious, educational and cultural life was loosened somewhat in the 18th century, before finally being broken when the Jesuit Order was abolished by the Pope in 1773, in the process handing back the entire Jesuit complex to the Wittelsbach royal family, before St Michael's joined the ranks of the destroyed and semi-destroyed during the Second World War. It, too, was restored, most recently between 1980 and 1983.

As well as St Peter's, the Frauenkirche and St Michael's, a host of other architecturally significant churches within Munich's inner city are worthy of note, including Friederich von Gärtner's twin-steepled Ludwigskirche (building-wise, finished 1837/38) at the end of Ludwigstraße, containing Peter von Cornelius's (1783-1867) masterful *Last Judgement* fresco. In addition, the imposing yellow façade of the Theatinerkirche at Odeonsplatz is a stark reminder of the Italian influence that held sway over the city in the mid-17th century, the impulse of which was provided by Duchess Henriette Adelheid of Savoy, the wife of Bavaria's Duke Ferdinand Maria.

Theatinerkirche (behind) and the Residenz (left) at Odeonsplatz open the city to Ludwigstraße

The Salvator Theatre was erected at a similar time, and when finished in 1654 became the first purpose-built court opera house in Germany. Unsurprisingly, considering the pre-eminence of religious morality in the city, its primary focus was the showing of Italian or 'serious opera'. In contrast, reflecting the lost influence of the pious Jesuits, by the reign of Max III Joseph, between 1745 and 1777, the royal family and court, took up something described as *Bauernwirtschaften*, which seemed to entail little more than wandering around the city in peasant attire for fun. Commensurate to this aping of peasants, the propaganda elements of the Italian operas that served merely to praise the ruler were gradually replaced with more credible alternatives.

Nymphenburg & the Residenz

One of the most significant legacies of Henriette's predilection for Italian architecture was the building of 'borgo delle nimfe', better known as Schloß Nymphenburg, on the outskirts of the city, under the direction of Italian Agostino Barelli (1627-1687). As is usual for such buildings, the start date for construction – 1664 – is far easier to locate than any end date, owing to the fact that once built, successive Bavarian rulers invariably order a renovation to the new style of the day. In 1701, for example, Max Emanuel ordered a great extension, which included side galleries and new residential buildings; in 1714, further buildings were completed and the palace's main façade was modernised to match the European fascination with all things French. Moreover. it is at Nymphenburg that Ludwig I's beauty gallery is to be found, including Lola Montez, the dancer responsible for his downfall in 1848, while Bavaria's most famous ruler, Ludwig II, of Alpine castle-building fame, was born there.

In contrast to most other historically significant buildings in Munich, Schloss Nymphenburg's location around five kilometres from Marienplatz saved it from the usual bomb damage at the hands of Allied air attacks in the Second World War. Today, Nymphenburg is Munich's second most frequented museum (after the Deutsches Museum), with around 567,000 people a year visiting the main palace, the extensive gardens and the glorious Amalienburg, a gift in the form of a palace, from Duke Karl Albrecht (from 1742 Emperor Karl VII, Munich's second Holy Roman Emperor) to his wife, Maria Amalia, and built by perhaps the court's greatest architect, Francois de Cuvilliés, and furnished in 1739.

Alter Hof: Munich's first royal residence, with legend-carrying Affenturm (Ape's Tower, right of centre)

The first Munich residence was the Alter Hof, which – though radically altered – still exists a few hundred metres from today's Residenz. Located on the north-east corner of the town, on the edge of the first town wall, archaeologists have dated the Alter Hof back to the 12th century. Up until the end of the 14th century, the castle complex initially consisted of a modest fortified construction on a slight elevation, surrounded by a ditch 11 metres wide and three metres deep.

Under Duke Ludwig II, the Alter Hof started to become the administrative centre for Upper Bavaria, more so under his successor, Rudolf I. Ludwig IV, one of Munich's most celebrated rulers, was born in the castle and legend has it that as a baby he was saved from a wild pig when an ape carried the terri-

Schloss Nymphenburg, by Bernardo Bellotto (Caneletto), 1761

fied child up one of the castle's towers (now known as the Affenturm, or Ape's Tower, though the legend seems to have altered to match the reconstruction of the castle through the centuries). Once the pig had disappeared, so the story goes, the benevolent ape took Ludwig to the safety of his room. The castle's high point was from 1328 under Ludwig's reign as Holy Roman Emperor, and

in contrast to previous emperors, who had tended to move from residence to residence around the realm, the Alter Hof was Ludwig's primary power base. Consequently, it received a renovation to match its importance, including the construction of a new church (Margarethenkapelle, later Lorenzkapelle) and was home to the imperial insignia, the imperial crown, sceptre, orb and relics. Although the construction has been altered over the centuries, it is home to Munich's oldest late-gothic vaulted cellar, which since 2007 has been a small but atmospheric museum explaining the the history of the Alter Hof and its changing role in the city through the centuries.

With the expansion of the city in the late 14th century, the Alter Hof was, to an increasing degree, no longer situated on the outskirts of the city, and therefore more exposed if attacked by an occasionally rebellious population. This prompted the building of a new residence, the moated Neuveste, started in 1384/5, further to the north-east, within the second city wall. In the 16th century, the highly educated and pious Duke Maximilian I saw the building of a more modern and structurally more impressive residence as part of his policy to manifest the message that he sat at the centre of a dynamic and powerful *Residenzstadt*, and, of course, that he should receive the concomitant title of 'elector' of the Holy Roman Empire, an honour not bestowed on Bavaria until 1632. Maximilian built adjacent to the existing Neuveste residence, which, through the centuries, was consumed by the new construction. The Residenz receive a partial but extravagant baroque renovation in the 17th century, witnessed occupying armies from Sweden and Austria and the inevitable exile of the royal family, until the Wittelsbachs' final deposition during the Bavarian revolution of 1918 saw it turned into a huge museum.

In 2007, a combined total of around 367,000 people visited the Residenz Museum and the Residenz Schatzkammer (treasury vault), while a recent peak of 570,000 was reached during the football World Cup year of 2006. Among the host of rooms open to the public, the Residenz's Antiquarium, measuring 70 metres in length, is one of the largest Renaissance halls north of the Alps and contains an impressive array of busts collected by Duke Albrecht V. The rococo-style Ancestral Gallery is – as the name suggests – a collection of portraits of contrasting quality of the Wittelsbach family. In addition, the Residenz is home to what is possibly the most ostentatious and impressive interior in Munich, the Cuvilliés Theater. Originally built by master architect Francois de Cuvilliés 'The Elder' between 1751 and 1755 for Elector Max III Joseph, it was meant to mirror the more enlightened, less pious and no longer Jesuit-influenced Munich. Though the style of the theatre was deemed to be out of fashion by the early part of the 19th century, a description of the theatre as a 'jewel of the rococo' was far from typical hyperbole. It was destroyed during the Allied

Right: the Renaissance-period Antiquarium in the Residenz remains a Wittelsbach homage to antiquity

bombings save some seating boxes and a handful of other significant artefacts, before it was rebuilt and restored to its glorious state in the following decades, with the most recent renovation completed in 2008.

The deposition of the Wittelsbach monarchy in 1918 has not, however, meant the entire removal of the Residenz from the centre of Bavarian power, geographically, at least: in 1994, the office of Bavaria's minister president (Bayerische Staatskanzlei), was controversially relocated to the renovated remains of the city's former army museum at the eastern end of the Hofgarten (Court Garden). The controversial location, cost and style of the new construction still periodically resurfaces, evidenced in German weekly magazine *Der Spiegel* asking in 2008 why it had to be so pompous and so costly at 450,000 euros a year.

Capital of Art

In 1782, Munich writer and historian Lorenz von Westenrieder (1748–1829) recorded in *Der Traum in Dreyen Naechten* (*The Dream in Three Nights*) a 'dream', in which he noted how Munich looked 300 years in the future:

> I was able to recognise the main streets and the two towers, which in silent majesty rose above the clouds – a glorious creation! But more than that, everything was strange and unrecognisable. I could no longer see the ramparts and the city wall that had surrounded the city, and in their place stood tiny buildings … How should I describe the impression that the glorious main streets made on me? There were no more tiny and often unclean side streets, where industries of every kind had been scattered about … I didn't see any very small houses next to large villas, and the informal garbling and disorder of many buildings was nowhere to be found.

Presient though Westenrieder's fictional dream proved to be, few could have predicted just how rapidly and how extensively Munich would be transformed. What had previously taken over 600 years to gradually evolve would in the 19th and 20th centuries be transformed by an art boom, new architecture and by huge city expansions that devoured outlying towns and villages. No one

The Alte Pinakothek holds one of the world's most impressive collections of 19th century art

did more to alter the Munich cityscape than Ludwig I, who is once said to have magisterially declared: 'I, the King, am art in Munich.'

Napoleonic-era Munich became the centre of a kingdom, initially propelled towards modernity by the relatively enlightened King Maximilian I and his modernising first minister, the French-influenced Maximilian von Montgelas. In simple terms, the plan was to create a modern capital city fit for a king, one that could measure up to other great German cities. Secularisation and the dispossession of church property freed up considerable space for renovation and rebuilding, most symbolically with the building of the Nationaltheater on the newly laid out Max-Joseph-Platz, adjacent to the Residenz, once the location of an imposing Franciscan cloister. Furthermore, the impact of the new regime's thinking could be discerned by the further dismantling of the city's defensive walls and battlements, and the laying out of the grand neo-gothic Maximilianstraße and the foundation of Maxvorstadt, a new urban centre just north of the Altstadt, both of which extended the city borders and were indicative of the changing nature of 19th-century Munich.

Though unable to compete with cities such as London, Paris and the increasingly powerful Prussian capital of Berlin in size and sheer industrial and economic might, Ludwig I's Munich came to personify the art metropolis par excellence, and by the second half of the century it was firmly established as the leading art centre in the German Empire and one of the greatest in Europe. Indeed, in contrast to the more centralised France and Britain, the dissipated nature of power in the post-Napoleonic German Confederation manifested a number of celebrated regional centres of art; and many of the artists were heavily influenced by trips to Italy, later in the century by training or working in Paris. The 1871 creation of the German Empire initially did little to change this, and arguably, for a time, unification accentuated artists' focus on the localities.

Germany's main centres producing art (rather than exhibiting art, of which there were many more) in the 19th century were Berlin, Dresden, Munich, all royal capitals, and Düsseldorf, all of which had their own art colonies, predominantly in idyllic, rural locations. But as Robin Lenman has shown in his superb *Artists and Society in Germany, 1850-1914*, one city stood out: 'In the second half of the 19th century,' he writes, 'not only Germany's but Central Europe's most important art-production centre was Munich.'

Shortly after Duke Maximilian I had taken the Bavarian throne in 1598, the royal art collection numbered over 3,000 objects, and included works by Albrecht Dürer as well as by Flemish, Italian, Dutch and French masters. Assiduous collectors of art as various Wittelsbachs proved to be over the next few centuries, on his abdication in 1848, Ludwig I bequeathed to Munich a cultural provenance far more significant than would have seemed conceivable at the turn of the century.

As well as grand streets, most notably Ludwigstraße with its extensive library and Ludwigskirche, there was Königsplatz, with architect Leo von Klenze's Glyptothek (the first public museum in Germany), which (reflecting the king's fascination with antiquity) today contains Greek and Roman collections of antiquities; a few hundred metres away, Klenze's Alte Pinakothek opened its doors in 1836, for which in 1827 Ludwig had purchased the impressive Boisserée Collection and a number of other old masters. As well as building on centuries of Wittelsbach collecting, the Munich royal line had inherited numerous works from family lines in Zweibrücken, Mannheim and Düsseldorf, while Ludwig also inherited the treasures from his father's Bavaria-wide secularisation measures of a few decades earlier. At its opening, the Alte Pinakothek

The Pinakothek der Moderne was designed to flood with natural light

held, according to Lenman, 'the world's largest Rubens collection' and many 'French, German and Italian old masters'. Destroyed in the Second World War, by 1957 it had been rebuilt in a similar style, and it today holds over 800 paintings and is renowned across the art world for its 14th to 18th-century masterpieces.

Directly opposite is the Neue Pinakothek, which originally opened in 1853 as a museum for contemporary art and was designed by Klenze's major rival, Friedrich von Gärtner. It was similarly destroyed during the Second World War and subsequently completely redesigned before opening in 1981 and counts as one of the most important museums of 19th-century art in the world. The Alte Pinakothek and the Neue Pinakothek are two of the principal museums comprising an area of the city known as 'Kunstareal München' ('Art Area of Munich'), which is located in Maxvorstadt, an area that includes the Ludwigs-Maximilian-Universität. The third major Pinakothek in this area is the 2002-opened Pinakothek der Moderne, superbly designed for a light-filled interior by Stephan Braunfels. It holds 20th- and 21st-century exhibits under the rubrics of 'art', 'paper', 'architecture' and 'design', meaning it is four museums in one. The newest museum in the area is the contrasting though equally impressive Brandhorst Museum, which opened in 2009. It was recently described by none other than the *Guardian*'s sometimes hard-to-please architecture and design critic Jonathan Glancey, thus:

> The painterly façades of Munich's new Brandhorst Museum are more than just a wonderful architectural flourish. Clad in a geometric coat of many colours, here is a building that looks like a giant abstract painting. This couldn't be more appropriate, since the Brandhorst's purpose is quite simple: it's a big, seductive container for the display of hundreds of contemporary paintings, sculptures and videos – including work by Andy Warhol, Joseph Beuys, Cy Twombly, Gerhard Richter, Bruce Nauman and Damien Hirst. Culturally, Munich is raising its game.

Munich's reputation as an art centre of import increased as the 19th century progressed, according to Lenman, due to the city's amalgam of the 'historical-monumental' painting style promoted by the Bavarian state and its official academy, and the 'popular-naturalistic' painting favoured by the Munich Art Union and bourgeois art buyers. The city's prestige was further enhanced by the appointment of venerated Realist painter Karl Theodor von Piloty (1826-86), a teacher at – later director of – the Munich Academy, and his colleagues Wilhelm Lindenschmit (1829-1895) and Wilhelm Diez (1839-1907). Such painters, plus its famous salon and international exhibitions, enticed hundreds of students from all over the world, including a number of Realists from the US in the 1870s. In addition, as shown by Maria Makela, in the 1850s Munich could offer artists in the city two unique exhibition spaces: the Kunst– und Industrieausstellungsgebäude (Art and Exhibition Building) constructed in 1845 opposite the Glyptothek on Königsplatz; and the Glaspalast, designed by August Voit for the 1854 German industrial exhibition, which was inspired by Joseph Paxton's Crystal Palace for London's Great Exhibition of 1851 (both, incidentally, destroyed by fire within five years of one another, in 1931 and 1936 respectively).

The 1869 art exhibition at the Glaspalast drew in over 100,000 visitors to see the 3,411 pieces on show, including Wilhelm von Kaulbach's (1804-1874) *Battle of Salamis* and Wilhelm Leibl's (1844-1900) *Mina Gedon*, as well as works by numerous French artists. The huge success of the 1869 exhibition attracted more artists, who flocked to Munich to train and work, while others arrived to purchase pieces or to merely soak up the atmosphere in such a thriving artistic centre. According to Makela, in 1886 there were 796 painters and 148 sculptors in Munich; by 1895 this had risen to 1,180 painters and sculptors, totalling around 13 per cent of all artists in Germany (Berlin, with four times the population, had 1,159). The total had risen to 1,770 painters alone in Munich by 1914, though many thousand more were by then in Berlin.

In the decades after German unification in 1871, the most popular artists of the time were treated as little short of celebrities, and as described by Matthew Jefferies they were often lauded as 'great men' or 'heroes', itself a reflection of a broader trend that it was great men who made history. The spirit of the age was perhaps best summed up by Munich-based painter Wilhelm von Kaulbach's comment: 'It is history we must paint. History is the religion of

The 2009-opened Brandhorst Museum, located in Munich's Kunstareal, or 'Art Area'

our age; only history is in keeping with the times.' This was exemplified by a comment by British painter John Lavery, a regular visitor to Germany in the late 19th century, who explained that 'the status of a painter was equal to that of a general in the army; he was covered with decorations at public functions and saluted as a person of distinction.'

Portrait painter Franz von Lenbach (1836-1904), one of Germany's so-called 'princely-painters', was one such artist awarded celebrity-like status as art became more identified with national destiny and greatness. Lenbach's status in the second half of the 19th century was such that he painted Chancellor Bismarck, the architect of German unification, around 80 times. And his villa, Lenbachhaus, at Königsplatz, is testament to his influence and wealth, more so as he commissioned the most influential Bavarian architect of the time, the seemingly ubiquitous Gabriel von Seidl, to build it (Seidl was also responsible for the Deutsches Museum and the Künstlerhaus (House of Artists), on today's Lenbachplatz, near the Stachus circus).

While Ludwig I promoted a host of artists, such as Lenbach, Wilhelm von Kobell (1766-1855) Peter Cornelius and Kaulbach, his successor, Maximilian II, was much more interested in promoting science. This heralded in the beginning of diminishing royal patronage of art and architecture, a process hastened under the reign of Ludwig II, who had relatively little interest in Munich or its artists, preferring instead to devote time to ever-more delusional Alpine building projects.

Secession

In the wake of Prussian-led German unification, the stock of local Munich artists rose dramatically as artistic success was used to compensate for the loss of Bavarian political influence vis-à-vis Berlin. Munich's rise to become Germany's pre-eminent art centre reached something of a high point between the 1860s and the late 1880s, culminating in 1888, the year of the city's most successful exhibition to date. Contemporaneously, however, Munich was already facing considerable difficulties in its effort to stay ahead of the pack. Reflecting Munich's transition since the more autocratic reign of Ludwig I, who invariably managed to prevail with his artistic inclinations, during the so-called 'regency' period, between 1886 and 1912, Prince Regent Luitpold had fewer resources with which to buy art. It was largely left to wealthy individuals and the state to make purchases, so much so that the famous Feldherrnhalle lions at Odeonsplatz, for example, were bought for the city by the brewer Matthias Pschorr, not by the Wittelsbachs.

In addition, Munich's less pronounced industrialisation in comparison to other German cities, instead focusing more on its role as an art and tourist location, paradoxically had a detrimental effect on it ability to maintain its position at the pinnacle of the German art hierarchy: fewer industrialists and entrepreneurs meant it had far fewer wealthy patrons and collectors able to partake in what was an increasingly expensive and sophisticated art market. In addition, Munich's rival of Berlin was raising its game. In 1886, it erected its own huge exhibition centre and its emerging image as an exciting metropolis gradually came to represent an attractive alternative to Munich.

With poor sales and criticism of bias in favour of modern and foreign work, Munich's third annual exhibition, in 1891, could not have been more different from that of the high point of 1888. In a list of reform proposals, it became clear that the majority of members of the Munich Artists' Guild wanted to sideline foreign artists in favour of giving local artists greater exposure at the exhibitions, regardless of merit. This led to Germany's first Secession, as 11 artists, including big names such as Franz von Stuck (1863-1928) and Fritz von Uhde (1848-1911), left the guild, thus destroying any façade of unity within the Munich art community.

Compared to the more 'rowdy' Glaspalast exhibitions, the Secession exhibition manifested a more subdued atmosphere. It also had fewer objects on display, while better lighting and modern hanging styles attracted more serious art purveyors. The work on display, however, was not radically different from the 1891 show that had given rise to the Secession in the first place. Both exhibitions were dominated by Naturalism, though Symbolism played a greater role in the Secession. The starkest difference between art at the first Secession and the 1893 Glaspalast exhibition was that finding the truly innovative works at the latter was, according to Maria Makela, like searching for 'proverbial needles in a haystack of dated paintings and insipid anecdotal pictures'. It seems that getting avant-garde works displayed was not the problem; locating them among the multitude of mediocrity on display was. Indeed, it did not take long for further secessions to develop from the original, a process that gradually spread across Germany, including Berlin in 1899. On the one hand, it is probably accurate to say that the Munich Secession engendered a much more diverse art environment, but on the other, as noted by Robin Lenman, on the eve of the First World War, 'the Munich Secession frankly described itself as a "bulwark against ultra-radical endeavours."'

While by the 1890s Berlin had all but caught up to Munich as an attractive location to make and sell art, Munich was still home to a highly diverse and vibrant array of artists and art scenes, with arguably the best yet to come, characterised by the term 'Bohemian Schwabing' (though in reality, many artists lived and worked in the adjacent Maxvorstadt area). A century earlier, Schwabing had been little more than a farming village, before in 1837 becoming the centre of Anton von Maffei's locomotive building works. By the 1890s it had been transformed into the innovative heartbeat of avant-garde Munich, seen as representing the polar opposite of the backward-looking neo-classicism of Ludwig I and the Realist and historicist paintings of later in the century. From the 1890s to the beginning of the First World War in 1914, three 'concepts' above all others came to the fore in Munich that made an impact across Germany and wider Europe: *Jugendstil*, *Simplicissimus* and most famously the Blue Rider group of artists.

Jugendstil & *Simplicissimus*

The emergence of *Jugendstil* was in a way heralded by Herman Obrist's (1863-1927) 'whiplash' design, which subsequently inspired August Endell's 1898 sweeping abstract relief that adorned the Hof-Atelier Elvira (destroyed in the war and now the location of the US consulate). *Jugendstil* in Munich could be said to be a derivation of two similar art forms of the period: it had elements of the Art Nouveau movement that was becoming popular in Europe, with sweeping, curving lines and natural forms, such as the stems of plants and flowers. It also displayed recognisable traits from England's late-19th century Arts and Crafts Movement, with its simpler, solid and more rectilinear forms. Moreover, while *Jugendstil* featured both abstract curves and cubic forms, it also foretold the 'industrial designs' of the twentieth century, and it is interesting to note that 21st-century Munich designer Konstantin Grcic cites the Art and Crafts Movement as influencing his highly regarded work.

The main bathing area of the Muller'sche Volksbad

The origins of European Art Nouveau are wide and varied, though the style principally emanated from Britain and France, but also from woodcuts from Japan, which were hugely popular throughout Europe in the 1880s and 1890s. Work by Munich-based artists Thomas Theodor Heine (partly inspired by Scottish art group the Glasgow Boys), Hugo Höppener (1868-1948; known as 'Fidus') and Franz von Stuck provided some indication of the new style to come. Similarly, two British magazines established in 1893, *Pall Mall* and *The Studio*, surely laid some of the ground for *Jugendstil*'s eventual emergence in Munich. As Timothy W Hiles has shown in his *Fin-de-Siècle Munich and the Origins of Simplicissimus*, incipient Art Nouveau works by Walter Crane, Alan Wright and Aubrey Beardsley appeared in *The Studio*, while in 1894 and 1895 many similar designs appeared in a competition ran by the magazine. Moreover, in 1887 Herman Obrist, who had struck such a chord with his seminal 'whiplash' design of April 1896, visited Britain and is thought to have seen work by the Glasgow Boys and artists of the Arts and Crafts Movement.

August Endell's dashing *Jugendstil* relief on the Hof-Atelier Elvira unfortunately did not survive Nazi taste censors; it was torn down to avoid Hitler having to see it when he visited Munich for a Nazi 'Blood and Soil' exhibition at the Haus der Deutschen Kunst in 1937. *Jugendstil* dramatically fell out of fashion after the First World War, and many façades adorning numerous Munich buildings fell into disrepair while others were pulled down or were destroyed during the Allied bombings in the Second World War.

A rediscovery of the city's *Jugendstil* heritage in the 1960s coincided with an initiative to rebuild the war-damaged Villa Stuck, the elaborately decorated villa on Prinzregentenstraße built at the turn of the century for artist Franz von Stuck. The result of this initiative is that after many careful renovations the city is home to some impressive examples of *Jugendstil* façades. When completed in 1898, the Martin Dulfer-designed Die Villa Bechtolsheim (1898) on Maria-Theresia-Straße became Germany's first ever *Jugendstil* house. The façade of the main building, with its linear clarity and characteristic *Jugendstil* reliefs, is more than matched by the gracefully decorated interior stairwell and iron banisters of the adjoining tower construction.

The area of Munich most densely populated with examples of *Jugendstil* buildings is Schwabing, the most famous of which is the façade of Ainmillerstraße 22, the so-called 'Jewel of *Jugendstil*'. This four-storey gold, green and red façade by German architect Ernst Haiger and Henry Helbig from the USA was renovated in 1983. Its more ostentatious façade is very much in contrast to the subtleties of Die Villa Bechtolsheim, highlighting that the style was far from uniform.

Arguably, the most impressive *Jugendstil* concept is the Muller'sche Volksbad, located on the shores of the Isar, within shouting distance of the Altstadt and metres from the Deutsches Museum. Designed by Professor Karl Hocheder, the baths were opened in May 1901, and the 50-metre clock tower-cum-water reservoir, with its blue clock face surrounded by a yellow background and white reliefs, betrays the elegant *Jugendstil* decoration of the interior. Largely undamaged by war-time bombing, and with just the mechanics being updated in the 1950s, the building has needed just the odd renovation to maintain its wonderful appearance.

Jugendstil, however, was always far more than just architecture and for some commentators it reached its high point in furniture, ceramics, porcelain and jewellery. Hence, the programme for the first *Jugendstil* exhibition, at the Glaspalast of 1897, stated that it placed its

> main emphasis on originality of invention and on the perfect artistic and technical execution of such artistic objects as fulfil the requirements of our modern life .... [This] excludes everything that appears as a thoughtless and false copy or imitation of past and foreign styles that is not abreast of the latest developments in modern technology.

These *Jugendstil* creations, therefore, were not one-off pieces for sale to the highest bidder, and the decorative and highly elegant furniture of Richard Riemerschmid (1868-1957) and Hermann Obrist are just two examples of artists whose *Jugendstil* designs were predominantly machine- rather than hand-produced. Many such designers were inspired to a degree by the idealistic Arts and Crafts concept of a 'community of craftsmen' designing pieces that though focusing on very high quality were widely available, which often meant produced in large numbers. While the social reform agenda of the movement should be taken seriously, it was never able to overcome the apparent contradiction that the primary proponents of *Jugendstil* were largely drawn from the bourgeoisie and the work itself was largely out of financial reach of members of the working class.

Nevertheless, the United Workshops for Art in Handicraft (Vereinigte Werkstätten für Kunst im Handwerk, which still exists) was set up to promote, market and produce *Jugendstil* products. And for a city that had hardly entered into the race of large-scale industrialisation, that the United Workshops employed around 600 people by 1907 is revealing. 'In its organisation and degree of mechanisation,' writes Kathryn Bloom Heisinger 'the Vereinigte Werkstätten seemed a miracle of modernism to contemporary critics and, by association, Munich a capital of art industry.'

Jugend (*Youth*), a weekly publication founded in 1896, was the most influential magazine to emerge alongside *Jugendstil*, and most probably lent its name to the movement. The magazine's publisher, Georg Hirth (1841-1916), came up with the name when at a viewing area named 'Jugend' on a trip to Hohenschwangau castle in the Bavarian Alps. Hirth, a progressive liberal, was also the proprietor of the 1896-founded *Münchner Neuesten Nachrichten* (the forerunner to today's *Süddeutsche Zeitung*). With *Jugend*'s distinctive covers and featuring, for example, new art, design and literature, Hirth's publication in retrospect came to be remembered as the mouthpiece of the *Jugendstil* movement. The journal, however, was subtitled *Illustrated Weekly for Art and Life* and it featured articles on politics, fashion and sport, and humour and parody were integral to the entire concept, while it was open to other art styles, not just *Jugendstil*. At its peak in 1900, *Jugend*'s circulation was as high as 300,000 copies sold each week, though by 1904 this had dropped to around 100,000, reflecting the meteoric rise and fall in popularity of the style itself.

Another magazine founded in 1896 soon became influential on an altogether different scale. *Jugend* contributor Thomas Theodor Heine and talented young publisher Albert Langen (1869-1909) cooperated on the weekly illustrated satirical magazine *Simplicissimus*, which was loosely derived from a classic novel of the Thirty Years War by German author Hans Grimmelshausen, entitled *The Adventuresome Simplicius Simplicissimus*. The concept was that just as the *Simplicissimus* character had exposed war in all its horrors, *Simplicissimus* would expose the misdeeds of the German Empire. *Simplicissimus* attracted some of the best authors and satirists Germany had to offer, including acclaimed playwright Frank Wedekind, Rainer Maria Rilke, Hermann Hesse (1877-1962) and Heinrich Mann, brother of fellow-contributor Thomas, perhaps Germany's greatest 20th-century writer, though it was often for the illustrations by Heine, Olaf Gulbranson (1873-1958) and Bruno Paul (1874-1968) that made the magazine so popular.

Iconic *Simplicissimus* dog designed by Thomas Theodor Heine

With Heine's iconic poster featuring a red bulldog on black background, his clever use of a devil figure and the magazine's caustic wit and biting parodies, *Simplicissimus* was frequently on the wrong end of the wrath of official censors. After an attack on Emperor Wilhelm II in 1898, this time for describing the monarch's trip to Palestine as a 'useless crusade', Frank Wedekind, the author of the offending article, was imprisoned for four months, while Langen fled in exile first to Zurich, then Paris, not deeming it safe to return until 1903. After also finding evidence that Heine had collaborated on the article, he too was imprisoned for six months. Inevitably, the effect was to greatly increase the popularity of the magazine and sales increased from around 15,000 to 85,000.

As with *Jugendstil*, *Simplicissimus* was a concept for a specific era, and its deterioration paralleled its embracing of an ever more nationalistic and chauvinistic tone, thus, fitting well with the prevailing trend in the years leading up to First World War. Between the wars, the magazine was no supporter of the Nazis, and it was no surprise to see it receive a forced Nazi makeover after 1933. Publication was temporarily stopped in 1944 and a new title of *Simpl* running between 1946 and 1950 was an attempt at reviving a once illustrious concept. A final attempt to recreate past glories was tried in 1954 before the ghost was given up in 1967.

The Blue Rider

As noted above, between 1887 and 1891 Munich architect Gabriel von Seidl built a palatial villa for the renowned artist Franz von Lenbach. Trusted portraitist of Chancellor Otto von Bismarck plus many other leading figures from the German Empire, by the late 1880s Lenbach, highly respected though he certainly was, had come to represent the conservative establishment that the Munich Secession had initially appeared to want to sideline. Similarly, just as the Secession now appeared increasingly to be little more than a caricature of its once progressive self, The Blue Rider (Der Blaue Reiter) emerged and soon became one of Europe's most innovative groups of artists.

Many of the artists who would later comprise the Blue Rider group had in fact honed their Expressionist styles in the hothouse atmosphere of *fin de siècle* Munich and though it should not be overstated had something to thank the Secession for in their emergence.

Russian-born Wassily Kandinsky arrived in Munich in 1896 and in 1900 won a place at Franz von Stuck's sought-after class at the Munich Academy, as did Paul Klee, a native of Switzerland. Similarly, Franz Marc, from Munich, also attended the Academy. Secession shows, such as the 1898 Symbolist exhibition featuring works from Russia and Finland, were probably visited by Kandinsky, and all the artists were well aware of the *Jugendstil* movement. Moreover, Maria

Makela highlights the initial 'subtle affinities between the essentially nature-oriented, lyrical and generally optimistic sensibility of the work exhibited at the Secession salons and that produced by Kandinsky, Marc and others of the Blaue Reiter group.'

Inevitably, however, artists looking to be more experimental grew weary of the increasingly backward-looking Secession exhibitions, encapsulated in a letter from Kandinsky to Gabriele Münter, his former student, later lover and Blue Rider colleague:

> I went to the Secession not without a little nervousness: but it wasn't completely unfamiliar to me, after all … Already in the first room I found the same [Franz von] Stuck. Everything exactly where it used to be … And only two new German artists, both insignificant … In half an hour I was done with the exhibition and gallery, and didn't even get tired.

And in 1901, an article by the Berlin art critic Hans Rosenhagen managed to conflate and hit both Lenbach and the Secession in one well-aimed shot:

> The Secession … appears to have utterly forgotten its essential objectives. For what is this so-called Donatello and Renaissance Art Exhibition, which has already taken place twice in the Secession's house, if not propaganda for Lenbach's ideas about the single true Art and a commendation for Munich's imitation industry?

The Blue Rider group was a loose group of artists who formed as a collective response to accusations that purchasing policies across Germany were far too focused on acquiring foreign works. Swiss-born Hugo von Tschudi (1851-1911), for example, newly arrived in Munich in 1909 from Berlin, where he had frequently clashed with Kasier Wilhlem II over his Impressionist and other – particularly French – modern art purchases, courted further controversy when he bought a van Gogh for Munich's Neue Pinakothek, upsetting traditionalists. Tschudi died in November 1911, but in the short period he was in Munich he had secured paintings of

Right: Wassily Kandinsky's *Munich-Schwabing With St. Ursula Church,* 1908

KANDINSKY
1908.

the quality of Van Gogh's *Vase of Sunflowers*, Manet's *Breakfast in the Studio* and Monet's *Bridge at Argenteuil*, plus others by Gauguin and Renoir.

Kandinsky's frustration with the conservatism of the Munich art establishment came to a head in December 1911 when one of his works was rejected for a city exhibition. Reinhard Piper, proprietor of Piper Press, met up with Franz Marc and then Kandinsky to discuss the artists' plan of publishing a manifesto outlining their artistic ideas. Winning the support of gallery owner Heinrich Thannhauser, the newly formed Blue Rider exhibited at his Munich gallery in December 1911 under the title of 'Exhibition by the Editors of The Blue Rider', which subsequently toured Germany. In total, 43 works were presented, including pieces by Kandinsky, Marc, August Macke and Münter, but also other artists, including Henri Matisse and Robert Delaunay. A second exhibition of the group's works was held at the gallery of Hans Goltz between February and March 1912, and this final exhibition also featured works by Picasso. The 150-page Blue Rider manifesto, *Blue Rider Almanac*, was a little slower to be produced than the exhibitions, not seeing the light of day until May 1912, but it is considered to be the first modern publication accompanying an art exhibition, which, of course, are nowadays so prevalent.

The Blue Rider legacy has been far reaching, with many major museums around the world eager to own work by group members, particularly Kandinsky. Immediately preceding the closure of Lenbachhaus in March 2009 in order to allow British architect Sir Norman Foster's practice to start on renovation work and the erection of a new adjoining exhibition building, the museum put on a spectacular Kandinsky exhibition. To the uninitiated, this might appear to be a touch paradoxical: one of the pre-eminent abstract artists of the 20th century appearing at Lenbachhaus, the home of the very person the likes of Kandinsky held up as a bastion of artistic conservatism. In fact, in the 100-or-so years since The Blue Rider's rise to prominence, Lenbachhaus has come to represent the most important location in the world for the group's works. In 1924, Lenbach's widow sold the villa to the city, and from 1929 it became home to the Städtische Galerie, or City Gallery. Most important in its development, however, were the donations of Gabriele Münter on her 80th birthday, in 1957, and in 1965 of Bernhard Koehler, whose combined generosity gifted numerous works to the gallery from Kandinsky, Marc, Klee and August Macke, as well as Münter herself.

That the Blue Rider is proudly held in high esteem by art goers is obvious from the 400,000 visitors to the 2009 Kandinsky exhibition, which was a collaboration between the two biggest holders of Kandinsky's work: Lenbach House and New York's Guggenheim. The exhibition successfully went on to be staged at Paris's Centre Pompidou, the city in which Kandinsky lived from 1939 till his death in 1944.

Critics tend to see Wassily Kandinsky as the leading light of the Blue Rider. Certainly, his radical use of colour and his preference for independent forms and lines were at the forefront in the development of abstract art. Art historian Rainer Metzger, in his *Munich. Its Golden Age of Art and Culture, 1890-1920*, rightly places Kandinsky on a similar level to writer Thomas Mann regarding worldwide reputations of Munich cultural figures.

Today, Munich is a city boasting over 80 art galleries of one sort of another, though it would be accurate to note that other European cities, particularly London, Rotterdam and Berlin, are nowadays far more celebrated for cutting-edge art and design than Munich is. In addition to its art galleries, the city has 56 theatres, 7 public orchestras and 41 museums, the overall quality of which undoubtedly adds considerable substance to the city's – admittedly often over-done – refrain of 'Munich: City of Culture'.

Jewish Munich

Former culture correspondent of German newspaper *Frankfurter Allgemeine Zeitung* Renate Schostack asserts, 'No other city, not Berlin, has a similar burdened and complex National Socialist past' than Munich. On her appointment as the paper's Munich correspondent, she recalls a colleague mumbling about 'loud corpses in the cellar', alluding to the perception that the city had much to hide and was not particularly well known for being up front about its Nazi past.

That was more than two decades ago. In a popular permanent exhibition at Munich's Stadtmuseum, entitled 'Typisch München!' (Typical Munich!), Munich presents itself as a city that manages to appear ultra modern (home of *Jugendstil* and capital of 'high-tech Bavaria') at the same time as appearing slightly kitschy and even backward-looking. Tracing the history of the city from the 12th century, the exhibition includes a substantial section on Munich and National Socialism. In addition to this, as noted in chapter 4, a permanent exhibition at the Stadtmuseum entitled 'Chiffren Der Erinnerung' is wholly dedicated to exploring the inextricable relationship between Munich and the rise of National Socialism.

A central tenet of Munich's long and difficult *Vergangenheitsbewältigung* ('coming to terms with the past') is the recent relocation of the city's Jewish community back into the centre of the city. This has also entailed a physical presence in the form of Jewish buildings, something that for many years after 1945 were conspicuous by their almost total absence. This was in stark contrast to the legacy of Nazi architecture around the city. The most obvious examples of the physical legacy of the Third Reich are the Haus der deutschen Kunst, now Haus der Kunst, which today functions as a successful art exhibition centre; and Königsplatz, encompassing the Führerbau, today Hochschule für Musik und Theater München, the NSDAP Administration Centre, now home to various cultural institutes under the title of Haus der Kulturinstitut, and Paul Ludwig Troost's now column-less Honour Temples (Ehrentempel) that commemorated the Nazi dead in the failed Nazi putsch of 1923.

In light of the destruction of Jewish reference points between 1933 and 1945, the other very important side of the coin of this Nazi legacy is the post-war role of the Jewish community in the city. Munich's principal synagogue after 1945 was hidden away in a nondescript building, off the impressively laid-out 19th century Gärtnerplatz, just outside the city's Altstadt. Security concerns meant heavily armed police were stationed across from the synagogue while inside (also guarded) the tight rooms of its small museum were utterly inadequate and more akin to a community in hiding rather than an integral part of city life.

The 2006-completed Jewish centre at St.-Jakobs-Platz, right in the heart of the city, somehow aptly adjacent to the city's own Munich Stadtmuseum, is a lot more open and accessible. Security is still apparent, but the atmosphere has been transformed, relaying a message proclaiming the Jewish community is no longer content to hide away on the fringes of Munich society. 'We are no longer in a time like the 16th and 17th centuries when Jews were living in ghettos,' Ellen Presser, head of Munich's new Youth and Cultural Centre, explains. 'In those days,' she says, 'a ghetto could be built from two sides. The question is whether the door is locked from the inside or the outside. On the one hand, if the minority is not wanted it's an impulse to close together. On

Marian Offman, CSU member of the Munich City Council

How did you come to be living in Munich?
My parents come from Poland but I was born in Munich, though when I was 10 months old we went to Canada. My uncle had come from a concentration camp – with my father he was the only survivor from my whole family – and he had TB. I got TB and because of this we went to Canada, where there were antibiotics. Here I would have died. We stayed there for five years and then we came back to Munich.

What motivated you to join a political party?
About 15 years ago I was at a memorial at Auschwitz for the 50 years liberation of the camp. I went there with a group of members of the Bavarian parliament, and I stayed with this group … for about one week. We went to the camp together, we saw everything; we cried there together, we mourned together. Me, the Jewish person, and they, the non-Jewish politicians from the CSU and from the SPD, all mourning for the murdered Jewish people. This, for me, was a sign that I could go into German politics, because I thought that if it is possible to mourn together with German politicians for the murdered Jewish people in Poland, in Auschwitz, then, it should be possible that I could go into German politics. That was my initial idea. Before, for me it was not imaginable to join a German party: it was '*die Partei*'. It reminded me of '*die Nazi Partei*'. Now I'm able to say *die Partei*, as the party I belong to. But it was a long way to get there.

Have you always been political?
I was always very political, even as a child. For example, in grammar school each year we saw a doctor and he asked me what I wanted to be. And I said: 'Bundeskanzler!' Of course, one of the main themes was the Holocaust, and I thought that if there were no weapons there could not be another Holocaust. So, I started my political way as a pacifist … I changed to the very left wing after this … My parents were very far from any religion. For them, the Holocaust was a sign that religion didn't work. But I got more and more in touch during the education of my children and my son's bar mitzvah, and I went to the synagogue each week. I got more religious myself and more conservative in my opinions. I changed from the left to conservative … My idea of being conservative is to be conservative like Thomas Mann: being conservative with a worldwide vision. Now I'm in the CSU and I belong to the liberal-left wing of the CSU.

How do you respond to critics who claim the CSU is too right wing?
A part of the CSU was right wing, but now the CSU is much more left than the CDU [the CSU's sister party]. It is the Christian *Social* Union. The social part is now very important. For example, I am the 'social-political' speaker for the CSU in Munich and I couldn't be in this party if it wasn't social and if it wasn't open to a certain kind of 'internationalism'. And of course against the radical right, the Nazis.

The Munich Stadtmuseum (City Museum) used to function as the city armoury and today sits opposite the new synagogue and Jewish museum

the other hand, it might be that the environment does not allow the exchange.' The aim of the relocation of the Jewish community back to the city centre, therefore, is precisely to facilitate an exchange: as visitors wander around the Altstadt, the open layout of St.-Jakobs-Platz encourages people to wander into the new kosher café or through the thoroughly modern glass-façaded shop that sits under the new Jewish museum. Splendid though the café and museum are, it is the new Ohel Jakob Synagogue that takes centre stage. Pivotally located in the middle of the square, relatively tightly flanked on either side by the Stadtmuseum and the aforementioned Jewish museum and café, which help create a multitude of vistas, the synagogue's imposing brick foundations initially seem to suggest some kind of fortification. This initial perspective diminishes as one's eyes rise upwards towards the much softer-looking cubed glass lantern structure of the roof and its lattice cover.

The Ohel Jakob Synagogue, opened in 2006

The relationship and interaction between non-Jewish Munich and its Jewish citizens is obviously not tension-free, and a degree of distrust from the latter towards the former is perhaps inevitable. Similar to other German cities Munich has its own small band of committed neo-Nazis, while it is an occasional location for neo-Nazi NPD (National Democratic Party of Germany) rallies. Indeed, in 2003 the return of the Jewish community to the heart of the city almost got off to the worst imaginable start when a neo-Nazi 'plan' was uncovered to detonate a bomb at the laying of the foundation stone for the synagogue. If such a plan had been carried out, police allege, it could have killed many members of the Jewish community, plus a host of Bavarian and Munich politicians and other dignitaries in attendance, including Christian Ude, the city's mayor, and the then Minister President of Bavaria, Edmund Stoiber.

The eventual 2006 opening of the Jewish centre was arranged to coincide with the anniversary of *Reichskristallnacht*, 9 November 1938, the day when Germany's Jewish community and its properties were openly attacked by rampaging Nazis, events that were instigated by Joseph Goebbels from Munich and seen by many as a turning point in the Nazi persecution of the country's Jews. For Ellen Presser, therefore, the opening of the new synagogue carried immense symbolic meaning and its name, Ohel Jakob Synagogue, is the same as that of its predecessor torn down prior to *Reichskristallnacht* on the direct orders of Hitler. 'On the day of the destruction of the synagogues of Germany,' says Presser, 'a new synagogue opened.'

In truth, in contemporary Munich society, the only real questions regarding the move back to the heart of the city for Munich's Jewish community was whether St.-Jakobs-Platz was the correct location. The situation today is that there is an increasing level of 'normalisation' in the relationship between Jews and non-Jews in the city. Jewish CSU city councillor Marian Offman explains: 'While being Jewish characterises my political world, ... I was born and raised in Munich and have a very close relationship to the city. I think my job is to normalise the relationship between Jewish Munich people and non-Jewish Munich people.' He stresses, 'I try to live a normal life as a Jew, as a Jewish German or a Jewish Bavarian, to show it is possible.'

Chapter 7

CITY OF BEER, CITY OF FOOTBALL

~

Part One: Beer

Tradition

The easiest method of highlighting its scale is to break it down into manageable figures. For example, in 2007: 69,406 hectolitres (6.9 million litres) of beer, 521,872 half chickens, 142,253 pairs of sausages and 104 oxen. Or perhaps it is clearer to quote the number of visitors: six million for the same year. These figures, of course, refer to the annual Oktoberfest, sometimes known as 'the world's biggest Volksfest', or 'the world's biggest beer festival'. After hitting 6.7 million visitors in 1990, rising to a high of 6.9 million in 1996, the number fell to 5.5 million in 2001, perhaps reflecting an unwillingness to travel in the wake of the 11 September terrorist attacks in New York. Since then, an average of around 6.1 million people have headed to Munich for the annual Oktoberfest.

Bavaria has a long history of being a brewing centre, in fact, the Weihenstephan brewery, based in Freising, just north of Munich, founded in 1040 by monks, proudly claims to be 'the oldest existing brewery in the world' (though this has recently been challenged by another Bavarian monastery brewery, at Weltenburg). Today, Bavaria is by far Germany's largest beer-producing state, while Munich is one of the most important brewing cities in the country. According to the 'Deutscher Brauer Bund' (German Beer Association), 1,302 breweries across Germany produced around 103 million hectolitres of beer in 2007. Almost half of the breweries – 627 (48 per cent) – are located in Bavaria, followed in second place by Baden-Württemberg with 182 breweries.

The exact period when beer began to be first brewed in Munich is unknown, though there is clear evidence that in the middle of the 13th century Duke Ludwig II ordered the founding of a royal brewery, which was a forerunner of the later and more famous royal Hofbräuhaus. In addition, sources show

A royal wedding celebration in 1810 later became known as the first 'Oktoberfest'. An early depiction was provided by Wilhelm von Kobell's 1811 painting entitled *Pferderennen (Horse Race)*

that Ludwig also gave permission to the Heilig-Geist monastery 'hospital' to distribute beer to Munich's downtrodden, poor and ill.

From the 13th century, the codification of feudal laws in Bavaria prescribed what beer should consist of and how much money from the proceeds had to be paid in tax. Nevertheless, it was wine rather than beer that was the favoured drink in Munich during the late Middle Ages, partly because of the often poor quality of beer, itself related to poor water quality and well-founded fears it could be a health hazard. This issue of beer quality is directly related to what is said to be the most famous food or beverage law in the world: the 'Reinheitsgebot', Bavaria's so-called 'beer purity law'.

The prescription of what could and what could not be included in beer was not unique to Bavaria. For example, a similar law was introduced in the free city of Nuremberg at the beginning of the 14th century, and which remained law until the 17th century. And in 1363 in Munich, 12 city patricians, including 11 members of the city council, formed a committee with the remit to ensure sufficient beer was available to the city's population and to ensure a good quantity, quality and price of beer. All three of these elements – quantity, quality and price – were similar to the Nuremberg beer law and the future Reinheitsgebot.

In 1447, city council regulations instructed Munich brewers to use only barley, hops and water when brewing beer, and this was followed up by 'official' confirmation in 1487 by Duke Albrecht of Bavaria. But a Bavaria-wide Reinheitsgebot was not introduced until a decree issued from Ingolstadt by Duke Wilhelm IV on 23 April 1516, which as well as setting the price of beer, also governed when beer could be brewed. Though it went through periods when the law was not adhered to, the 1516 Bavarian Reinheitsgebot remained law in Bavaria for centuries and was eventually incorporated into German law following unification in 1871. It was only a 1987 European Court of Justice ruling, stating, 'The German designation "bier" and its equivalents in the languages of the other member states of the community may therefore not be restricted to beers manufactured in accordance with the rules in force in the federal republic of Germany,' that finally seemed to have done for the over 450-year-old law. Though it was clear that the Reinheitsgebot did not adhere to European competition law, not to be defeated, the German government passed a law that stated beer made within Germany and outside the old Reinheitsgebot laws could not be called 'beer'. Obviously, as a marketing tool the ability to point to the 'purity' of one's beer is a huge advantage, though it remains controversial due to the fact that beers made within Germany that do not adhere to this specific law (for example, if they contain equally 'pure' ingredients though not the three stipulated of barley, hops and water) can on the surface appear less than wholesome.

Though it was only in the 19th century that Munich began to gain a wider reputation as renowned centre of beer, it owes its long tradition as a brewing centre to Duke Wilhelm V, famous for his piety, his anti-Protestantism and for abdicating in 1598 due to his inability to cope with Bavaria's expanding mountain of debt. As well as being the regent who took the lucrative Munich salt monopoly for his own coffers, it was Wilhelm who in 1589 had the Hofbräuhaus, or royal brewery, created, the forerunner of today's famous beer cellar of the same name. Prior to Wilhelm creating his own court brewery in Munich (he owned others around Bavaria), his court often imported beer from across the Holy Roman Empire, which was expensive, time consuming (taking, for example, four days just to reach Munich from Nuremberg) and incurred the risk of spoilation. Finished in 1590, the Hofbräuhaus was erected not far from the former royal residence, the Alter Hof, a few minutes' walk from today's Residenz. Wilhelm's successor, Maximilian, was a good deal less extravagant about spending money and made considerable effort to reduce the state's debt. As a way of ensuring an increase in income, in 1602 Maximilian forbade anyone else in Bavaria except his breweries from brewing Weißbier (wheat beer, which, due to the process of 'top fermenting', escaped the sometimes-elastic Reinheitsgebot), in effect creating a Weißbier monopoly for himself. In addition, as well as building a larger Munich brewery complex in 1606, which later became home of the Hofbräuhaus at Platzl, a series of Weißbier breweries were erected around Bavaria. The lucrative Bavarian Weißbier monopoly was only removed when the reform-minded Elector Karl Theodor dismantled it in 1798, while his successor, the future King Maximilian I, had all the royal breweries sold off, with the exception of two: one in the grounds of Schloß Schleißheim on the edge of Munich; and the second was Munich's Hofbräuhaus.

Beer Riots

Alongside often poor quality, the price of beer in Munich proved to be a perennial problem that was disputed between breweries, landlords of *Wirtshäuser* (pub-restaurants) and the drinking public. As seen in chapter 5, the quality of Munich's water supply and with it the quality of beer was eventually addressed by Max von Pettenkofer, who, by the 1870s had transformed Munich from one of Germany's least sanitary cities into a model of hygiene. Beer prices, however, were a different challenge altogether. While riots over beer prices had never previously seemed likely to cause the fall of a Bavarian ruler, in the decades after the final defeat of Napoleon in 1815, monarchies across Europe were particularly vigilant about public protests of any sort, more so after the 1830 July Revolution in France. The primary worry was that a protest against beer prices in Munich would be the catalyst for wider demands.

In the 1830s, Munich's beer barons were, it appeared to the city's population, disdainful about public concerns about the quality of the city's beer and beer prices as they ostentatiously displayed their wealth in the form of grand villas and luxurious carriages. Indeed, by the mid-1830s, ten of Munich's tax payers were brewers. The possibility of beer riots was caricatured by a correspondent for a French newspaper when he reported, 'The Bavarians are a rough but good-natured people, and nothing can really move them to rise up and rebel. But if someone were to take away their beer, then there would be a wild revolt.' The first of Munich's great beer riots started on 1 May 1844, a year after terrible crop failures across much of central Europe had piled misery on the population in the form of hugely inflated grain prices, with the concomitant effect of higher beer prices. Political agitation was already very much in the air as the influx of people from rural to urban areas started to change the relationship between town and country. And though Munich may not have been the centre of large-scale industrialisation, the city was certainly not immune to demands from an incipient industrial working class searching for better pay and conditions. The May protests against a hike in the beer price took the form of violence aimed at the brewery buildings, with the Munich city chronicler recording, 'All the window frames in the Löwenbräu house were battered down with great force, and the huge Pschorrhause, the Wagnerbräu, the Augustinerbräu were all wrecked.' Similarly, Bavarian civil servant Franz Xaver Gabelsberger noted,

> The revolution against beer [prices] is happening – if one can call it that – with Bavarian composure, so that except for the pubs, … nobody else's property has been damaged or put at risk. In the houses of the brewery owners, up to the third floor there are no remaining doors, drawers, tables or chairs, no ovens, no clocks, no cutlery.

On 2 May, Princess Hildegard was preparing for her wedding day (set for the next day) with her court ladies with increasing trepidation about the possibility of further disturbances. Again recorded by the city chronicler, a fearful mob formed in order to attack various brewery-related targets, just at the same time as the bride's wedding procession rode past. All of the stones and rocks meant for the windows of brewery property at once disappeared into pockets in order to allow the participants to applaud the princess, proof, according to the loyal chronicler, of the high esteem Munich's population held for the Wittelsbach royal family. Nevertheless, further rioting erupted, before the brewers decided they had seen enough and on 4 May they gave in to demands and dropped the price of beer. The cost had been over 30 breweries destroyed, one person dead, 10 policemen injured and 142 people arrested.

Four years later, few – if any – lessons appeared to have been learned by the brewers. In the wake of the abdication of King Ludwig I in 1848, the newly crowned King Maximilian II immediately ordered the lowering of the price of beer to four kreuzer. Brewers, thinking they knew better, quickly raised the prices again, which set off a series of small beer riots, culminating around the time of the 1848 Oktoberfest with the biggest beer riot the city had ever seen. With a slogan of, 'We want the beer for four [kreuzer],' on 17 October protestors along with members of the military set out for brewery property. Though there does not seem to have been much evidence of political demands from the swelling number of people in Munich, this was not the case in other cities at this time, where various economic and political demands were central to popular protests. The result, in Munich at least, was success: the price of a Maß beer was set at four kreuzer.

The last of the so-called great Munich beer riots was in 1910, and again it was a public protest against rising beer prices. Again it was directed at local brewers and landlords, though this time the price rise had been determined by a hike in the price of malt across the whole of the German Empire, not just Munich. Breweries and pubs were attacked and set on fire, with the usual result, as announced by brewer Joseph Bachmeier: 'That's enough,' he said. 'From tomorrow the price of beer will be served again at the old price.'

While the effectiveness of Munich beer riots had hardly changed in over half a century, during this time the Munich brewing industry had been transformed. In 1840, there were 40 breweries in the city, by 1860 this had fallen to 25, dropping to just 18 in 1870. As seen, just as in other areas of the modern economy, this contraction was predicated on the most powerful brewers buying up smaller, weaker ones. Only seven breweries in existence at the grounding of the German Empire in 1871 were still in existence by 1945. The others had been taken over or had gone to the wall. This had the effect of considerably weakening the diversity of Munich brewing, but it also had the effect of strengthening the surviving firms.

Today, though some small independent Munich breweries still exist, the city is dominated by six huge concerns that comprise the Verein Münchener

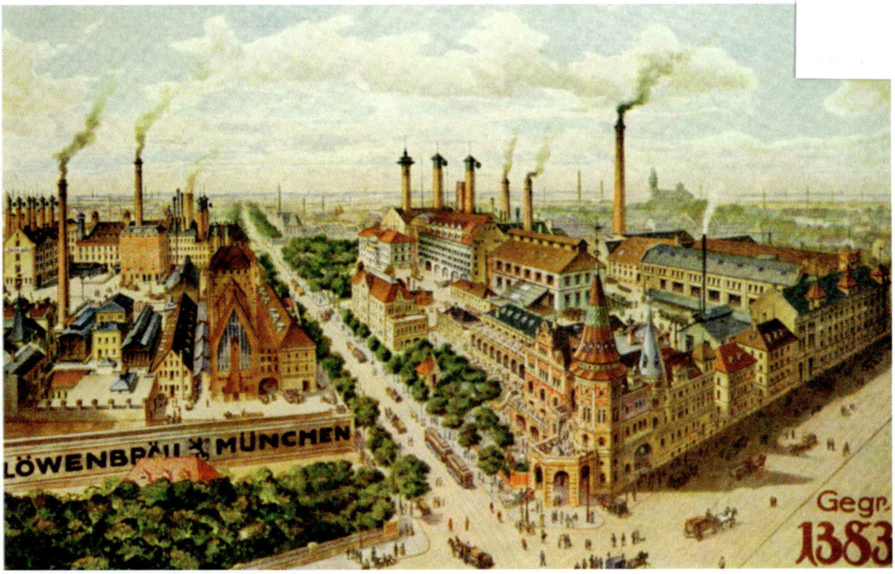

The extensive Löwenbräu brewery, Nymphenburger Straße, 1910

Brauereien (Munich Brewers Association): Augustiner-Bräu, Hacker-Pschorr, Löwenbräu, Paulaner, Spaten-Franziskaner and, reflecting that it is owned by the state of Bavaria, the Staatliches Hofbräuhaus in München. With the exception of the Hofbräuhaus, and less so Augustiner, however, this is only half the story as most of the breweries are subsidiaries of larger concerns and struggle to be described as German owned, never mind Munich owned (in fact, Löwenbräu and Spaten-Franziskaner are part-owned by the same parent company, the highly unimaginatively named AB InBev, currently the 'world's largest beer maker', according to the *Wall Street Journal*).

Regardless of the realities of who exactly owns the breweries, the city derives huge economic benefits from them, while Munich has a well-deserved reputation as home to a veritable honeycomb of distinguished beer halls, atmospheric restaurants and pubs, and most popular of all countless beer gardens, all predominantly selling 'Munich' beer. The ubiquitous Munich beer garden has arguably the city's greatest patron, King Ludwig I, to be grateful for its existence. In the 1820s and 1830s, Munich's rapidly expanding population was consuming greater quantities of beer. Prior to adequate cooling systems, in

A delivery of beer from the Spaten brewery, around 1920

the warmer months of the year, the beer was prone to go off. To counter this problem, as early as 1724, Munich breweries had taken to storing their produce in cellars near the tree-shaded and cooler shores of the Isar. It seems that over time, local residents had taken to taking a Krug (beer glass) to these Isar beer cellars in order to buy a Maß beer and hang about under the shade of the chestnut trees while drinking. Naturally, rudimentary bars, comprising little more than a few benches and tables, were erected, which attracted increasing numbers of people.

Landlords of Munich's growing number of *Wirtshäuser* were less than impressed with this direct selling of beer, prompting Ludwig I to rule that the Isar beer cellars could continue to sell beer, but they could not sell food. Importantly, however, if people wanted to eat while enjoying a beer, they could, he decreed, take along their own food, a tradition that Bavarian beer gardens enjoy to this day.

Oktoberfest

While many Münchners nowadays consider the 'world-famous' Hofbräuhaus as somewhat kitschy, something primarily for tourists, the contrast to the population's attitude to the much more popular Oktoberfest is stark. '*Wiesn*' is the Bavarian name for the Oktoberfest, and it is derived in part from the area where the festival takes place: the Theresienwiese, named after the future King Ludwig I's soon-to-be wife, Therese von Sachsen-Hildburghausen, plus the German word for 'meadow', *Wiese*. The first Oktoberfest took place to celebrate Ludwig and Therese's wedding in 1810, at a time when Bavaria was still embroiled with Napoleon's quest for European hegemony. Two years later, 30,000 Bavarians lost their lives during Napoleon's disastrous Russia campaign, and this fed into the recognition that a Bavarian national event might help draw the population closer to the Wittelsbach royal family. Indeed, the instrumentalisation of the past in events such as the Oktoberfest, with obligatory *Tracht* (traditional clothes), and the Landshuter Hochzeit (Landshut Royal Wedding, a four-yearly re-enactment originating in 1903 of a 1475 royal marriage) have been integral in the construction of Bavaria's founding national myths and particularly fed into notions of *Heimat*, which contributed to the implantation of a common identity on disparate people under the banner of 'Bavarians'.

Recognising the advantages of promoting the festival as a national occasion for the people of Bavaria, from 1825 Ludwig I initially attended the Oktoberfest very publicly and even handed out prizes to schoolchildren for poems they had written. His opinion was that, 'National festivals particularly please me. They articulate a national character, which is passed on to children and the children of children.'

Early Oktoberfests were more about horse racing than about beer, food and other forms of entertainment, and racing featured up until 1913 and again between 1934 and 1938. The original idea of combining wedding celebrations, a 'Bavarian national festival' and horse racing had probably come via a Major Dall'Armi of the Bavarian National Guard. Dall'Armi himself recorded that the 1810 festival 'was started with a holy mass and field music in the Burgersaal at nine in the morning.' It was followed by a procession of military personnel and musical bands to the festival area, where as many as 40,000 people eagerly waited for the royal family to take up its position on a raised platform on the edge of the horse track, thus, the centre-point of the whole festival.

The first festival began on 12 October and ended on the 17th with a great horse race. Though not originally envisioned as a yearly event, in October 1811, a second festival took place, at the newly named 'Theresens Wiese', lasting for two days and setting the festival as an annual event (though it has been cancelled a total of 24 times, mainly due to war, the first time as early as 1813, and in the cholera years of 1854 and 1873) to take place around the date of the king's Namenstag, in mid-October. These plans, however, were quickly altered when it was realised that King Maximilian I much preferred to go hunting on this day, which meant that from 1815, the festival date was altered to take place on the first Sunday in October, before it was shifted to late September in the hope of better weather.

Whether food and drinks were on sale at the first ever festival is disputed, though Fritz Fenzl and Richard Bauer have convincingly shown both were indeed available. Regardless of what was available inside the festival area, it seems that for the wider celebrations for his son's wedding, on 13 and 14 October 1810 King Maximilian was happy enough to provide at four locations around the city, in total and free of charge, 32,065 bread rolls, sizeable quantities of Swiss cheese, roast mutton and sausages, plus 352 hectolitres of beer and four hectolitres of white wine. It did not take many years, however, for entrepreneurial-inclined residents of the city to realise that a proverbial goldmine was to be had at this huge event, and soon rules were drawn up to allow only a limited number of food and drink sellers (with a small charge for the honour). By 1824, 31 landlords and brewers were approved to sell at the Oktoberfest, though today as a 'Munich beer festival' it is dominated by the six big Munich brewers.

In the early years, which brewers and landlords could sell at the Oktoberfest was down to the drawing of lots, though they rejected city council requests to use standardised huts in which to house their customers, much preferring their own wooden contraptions. A further milestone in the festival's history was reached in 1818 when Anton Gruber won approval to provide entertainment, such as carousels, swings and seesaws. With entertainment, beer, food and incipient tent-like constructions, the basic elements were in place that characterise today's festival. By 1835, 100,000 visitors were consuming

Die schöne Coletta (*The Beautiful Coletta*) is a painting of Coletta Möritz (1860-1953), who worked in a Munich beer hall. The image soon became the idealised vision of the Munich beer hall waitress (painting by Toni Aron, 1880)

240,000 Maß of beer, numbers only likely to increased with the construction of the railway line from Augsburg to Munich in 1839 making travel to the city from regions across Bavaria and further afield far easier. Indeed, the 1840 festival had to be shifted back a week to cope with the numbers. By 1862, the *Festchronik* (Festival Chronicle) was reporting, 'Like no other year, the influx of foreigners this year has taken on extraordinary dimensions ... Many hundreds of foreigners could not find accommodation and had to spend the night without a roof, while some stayed in cafes and pubs, others on the street, even though it was bitterly cold.'

This depiction has hardly changed in the near 150 years since then. In the intervening years, in addition to the development of modern transportation, Carl von Linde's refrigeration machines and Max von Pettenkofer's hygiene measures helped pave the way for the further development of Munich as a beer city of repute. And just as in the realm of Munich politics, industry and art, towards the end of the 19th century the Wittelsbach royal family played an ever-diminishing role in the city's beer industry and in the Oktoberfest. Indeed, never feeling comfortable in Munich, it is no surprise that from 1874 until his death in 1886, the never-popular King Ludwig II did not bother attending the festival. Though Prince Regent Luitpold revived the practice of the head of the Wittelsbach family attending the festival, the days of great royal patronage had long since ceased (in fact, the city authorities had taken over the festival organisation as early as 1819). The last visit of the Wittelsbach royal family to the Oktoberfest in an official capacity was King Ludwig III's visit in 1913, with no festival the following year – even with already constructed beer tents – due to the outbreak of the First World War shortly before its start. The most significant event at the Theresienwiese in the next four years was when on 7 November 1918 thousands of people gathered to hear Kurt Eisner and other left-wing revolutionaries speak, subsequently launching the Bavarian revolution. The Oktoberfest was again halted by war in 1939, not starting again until 1948, and in 1950 Munich mayor, Thomas Wimmer, started the tradition of the mayor opening the first cask of beer, the Oktoberfest *Anzapf'n* (the tapping of the first beer keg).

The festival experienced its worse ever incident on Friday 26 September 1980 when a bomb was exploded at the main entrance-exit area at around 10.30 pm, the very time when most people would be leaving the festival. Twelve people were killed by the explosion at the scene, a thirteenth died later, while around 250 were injured, over 200 seriously. Coming just eight years after the murder of 17 Israeli athletes while attending the Munich Olympics, the city was once again making headlines around the world for tragic reasons. It transpired that among the dead was the 21-year-old student Gundolf Köhler, a member of the banned neo-Nazi Wehrsportsgruppe Hoffmann. A hugely controversial investigation claimed the bomb had been the work of Köhler alone, a conclusion critics still deem far from convincing. As recently as 12 May 2009, the *Süddeutsche Zeitung* carried an article reporting renewed calls for further investigations into the alleged role played by far-right accomplices of Köhler. In addition, there have also been accusations that Bavarian authorities were far too concerned with getting the festival running again, which, the very next day it was, though the festival did eventually close for a day of mourning on 30 September. The day prior to the opening of the 1981 Oktoberfest, a memorial to the dead was unveiled at the festival entrance, adjacent to where the bomb had exploded.

Since the advent of the *Wirtschaftswunder* in the late 1950s, the Oktoberfest has became the place to be seen for the celebrities and socialites, often from beyond Germany, including film, TV and pop stars, not forgetting the yearly visit from the lederhosen-clad Bayern Munich footballer players. In addition, economically, the Oktoberfest has been a pot of gold to the city for decades. A report commissioned by the Tourist Office of the City of Munich in 1999/2000 came up with some telling conclusions: 'The economic value of the Munich Oktoberfest totals almost 954 million euros.' This includes, during the 16 days it runs, a huge 449 million euros directly at the festival as well as a further 205 million euros in the city. The survey also reveals that 72 per cent of visitors came from Bavaria, 60 per cent were local to Munich, with 15 per cent coming from abroad, predominently from Austria, Switzerland and France, while the rest of the EU, the USA, Australia and New Zealand were well represented. Perhaps most significant was that around 71 per cent of people visited Munich purely for the Oktoberfest, which on the one hand would certainly do nothing but reinforce stereotypical images that Munich is full of strange beer-drinking and lederhosen-/dirndl-wearing people; and on the other probably means many of these Oktoberfest visitors see little more than the inside of a hotel room and the inside of a beer tent.

Building a Football Culture

Picture the scene: 6 July 1954, a barely reconstructed Marienplatz, centre of a city still very much bearing the scars of its near destruction, pulsating with raucous cheers and songs emanating from an almost disbelieving crowd: nine years after the end of the Second World War, with thousands of German soldiers still waiting to be repatriated from Soviet prisons; with the West's default position still wary and often disparaging of most things German; with the *Wirtschaftswunder* still in its embryonic stages and still to make a sizeable impact on West German citizens; with deprivation, in everything from foodstuff to clothing to inadequate health care, all too evident; with all the physical signs of a defeated nation still apparent, exemplified by the countless ruins of centuries' old former architectural gems; and with the shame of the most destructive war in history reflected in the voices of foreign occupiers on German streets, in bars, cafés and cinemas, Germany's fairy tale-like victory over the favourites, the best team in the world, namely Hungary, to win the football World Cup provided an easily comprehensible ecstatic release. Cathartic would be an understatement. That the victorious team of the so-called 'Miracle of Berne' (*Das Wunder von Bern*) would be travelling north east from the Wankdorf Stadium in Switzerland seemed too good an opportunity not to seize. Germany's heroes were invited to the Bavarian capital to take the acclaim of the city's adoring population, thousands of which had cheered the players as they entered the city, culminating at Munich's Marienplatz. The *Münchner Merkur* newspaper recorded that the players had been transformed into 'idols' for millions of children whilst also comparing the players to 'film stars'. The report goes on to highlight that this adulation meant the children waiting in Munich's Altstadt went to any length to grab a good vantage point with which to catch a glimpse of their new heroes: 'At Marienplatz' reports the newspaper, 'children sit on the sculptures, in front of the adults … The throngs of onlookers climb higher and higher up the scaffolding.' Photographs from the celebrations at Marienplatz vividly bear this out, showing a heaving mass of people straining to catch a glimpse of the players. The *Münchner Merkur* reports an imaginary conversation revolving around police efforts to protect what is in effect a

Fans packed at an as yet not rebuilt Marienplatz waiting for the victorious 1954 football World Cup winners to emerge from the Munich Rathaus.

building site from swarms of people. The conversation concludes: 'Just enjoy it! We've not had much that we can be happy about lately.'

Prior to the 1960s, World Cup aside, Munich football fans certainly had little to be 'happy about'. The emergence of football in Germany as a game that one recognises today, with two teams of eleven and a set of rules, emerged wherever groups of British men were located, either studying or working. Football started to get a foothold in Germany in the late 1870s and early 1880s, at this stage primarily in the Bremen and Hanover areas. Arguably (and regardless of the dates attached to the names of many German clubs, which often depict when a particular parent sports – or 'gymnastics' – club was founded, not the football arm), the first real German football club was FC Germania Berlin, founded in April 1888. The first game in Munich did not take place until 1889, and it did not even feature a Munich team due to the city not having a single club at the time.

Elisabeth Angermair traces the first Munich football club to 5 September 1896 with the foundation of Terra Pila, 'earth' and 'ball' in Latin, which was part of a 'club for grass sports' (*Verein für Rasensportarten*). In 1899, it was renamed as the Münchner Fußball-Club von 1896, or Munich Football Club of 1896. Though historians have not found any substantial evidence to verify it, and in a fabulous reflection of the artistic vogue of the time, an FC Nordstern claimed in a letter with a *Jugendstil* letterhead that it rather than Terra Pila was in fact the 'the oldest football club in Munich'.

It was after the First World War, however, that football in Munich, indeed across Germany, really took off. In contrast to England, where the First Division was a league contested on a national basis, there was no national league in Germany, just regional leagues, from which the best teams would contest an end-of-season play-off to become German champions. From its inception in 1903, no Munich team proved itself good enough to become national champions until Bayern Munich won the competition in 1932, a singular success, hardly portentous of the club's transformation in the 1960s into Germany's most successful and wealthiest club. Founded in 1900, FC Bayern were born out of a dispute with MTV 1879 (Männerturnverein München von 1879), which had refused its football players permission to join an umbrella organisation, the South German Football Association (Verband Süddeutscher Fußballvereine). The players walked out in 1900 and formed their own club, Bayern Munich (Fußball Club Bayern München).

Although many general sports clubs from this time distanced themselves from the increasingly popular but 'rough' sport of football, Bayern were only one of a number of teams in the Munich area. MTV, for example, continued with a football arm after Bayern Munich's secession, while in 1899 FC Bavaria was formed, the same year as Turnverein München von 1860 (Gymnastics Club Munich from 1860, later known as TSV von München 1860), significantly – at least for 1860 fans – a year before their soon-to-be great rivals Bayern Munich. It is these two teams that survive today as the most historic and successful of Munich football clubs. Just as Bayern Munich were conceived from MTV, 1860 were merely an arm of Munich's biggest sports club, Turnverein von 1860. In 1910, the umbrella sports club of 1860 celebrated its 50th anniversary, though the football arm was just over a decade old. As the biggest sports club in Munich, in addition to football and gym sports, 1860 also comprised mountain climbing (1901), swimming

(1903), skiing (1907), hockey (1911) and 'strength events' (weight lifting and wrestling, for example, 1912). Today, these sports are supplemented *inter alia* by basketball and bowling, as they are similarly for Bayern Munich.

After three years of training, 1860's first competitive match was played on 27 July 1902 against 1. Münchner Fußballclub von 1896, which they lost 4-2, while on 21 September of the same year, they lost a first ever game against Bayern Munich 3-0.

With few specific football pitches across the city, Munich football clubs trained and played at a variety of places, two of the most popular locations being a grassy area of the city called Schyrenwiese and also on a southern section of the Theresienwiese, more famous as home of the Oktoberfest. MTV branched out into the Munich suburbs and regularly played at Gräfelfing, while in 1908 1860 secured a playing area in Giesing, which in 1911 became the club's official – and later heavily mythologised – Grünwalder Stadion home.

The foundation of Bayern Munich actually took place in a pub named Gisela in the Schwabing area of the city. In these early years Bayern played at a number of locations in Schwabing, Munich's famous artists' quarter, aiding the oft-made claim that the club was historically at one with this most bohemian part of Munich. After amalgamating with another Schwabing club, Bayern remained in the area when moving to Karl-Theodor-Straße, before moving again in 1907 to a location just off Leopoldstraße, where they built Munich's first ever covered stand for spectators.

Predominantly since the meteoric rise of Bayern Munich in the mid-1960s, many German football fans have attempted to portray 1860 as Munich's genuine 'workers' club', in contrast, so the story goes, to bourgeois Bayern Munich. In fact, as Anton Löffelmeier has shown, this image is a myth. How could it be anything but, when in January 1905 Prince Ruprecht, son of Prince Ludwig, future King Ludwig III of Bavaria, was named as the sporting club's patron while military officer cadets acted as sports instructors for young 1860 members? Though many early club membership records have been lost, Löffelmeier's research – particularly relating to membership contributions and records of people celebrating long club membership – shows that '1860 run in the tradition of the big bourgeois sports clubs of the 19th century.' before concluding that 'the classification of … 1860 as a "workers' club", even during the club's first 50 years of its existence, … is incorrect.'

In its early years, participation in football was, therefore, primarily a preserve of Munich's middle classes, with students and employees the real pioneers. Indeed, an early Terra Pila squad of twelve comprised five students, two state employees (from the postal service and the railways), three involved in the banking/insurance sector and two professional tradesmen. This make-up was pretty typical for the bourgeois origins of Munich football, with colour provided by further players before the First World War including academics, apothecaries, a film director and an opera singer.

The prime consideration for Munich's clubs before 1914 revolved around the rather modest aim of becoming the best club in Munich. The inaugural Munich Championship (Münchner Meisterschaft) of 1901/02 was won by Bayern Munich, as it was until MTV won the title in 1905. From 1907, under the auspices of the new Münchner Verband (part of the South German Football Association), Munich clubs competed for the Munich Regional Championship (Münchner Bundesmeisterschaft), which Bayern Munich won until 1860's success in 1909.

A measure of the quality – or lack – of Munich teams can be gauged from the fact that no team from the city qualified for the German national Championships prior to the First World War. Bayern Munich had proved themselves to be the best team in Bavaria in 1910/11 but were unable to make the leap of class to succeed in qualifying as South German Champions, though the club's relative success was an indication of the improvements top Munich clubs were making. But in a Germany increasingly characterised by the question of its geo-political role in the world, football was not ready to provide much of a fillip to German national pride. In December 1911, Munich hosted its first international game, during which 6,000 fans saw Germany lose 4-1 against Hungary. The *Münchner Neueste Nachrichten* newspaper conveyed an upbeat report, stating that 'Our German team played well. One could see in every man the existence of determination and ability.' Before adding that more or less everyone was inspired by the 'responsible' way that the team played, though even with these 'recognisable efforts, there was no real system on which to lay the foundations of the game.'

As a relatively still inexperienced footballing city, therefore, Munich clubs welcomed taking on better teams from across Germany, such as in 1905 when South German champions Karlsruher FV arrived, while Munich teams travelled to Dresden as well as abroad to Bohemia, Austria and Switzerland. Most prestigious of all were the visits by English league clubs, such as Sunderland in 1909, Blackburn 1910 and Middlesbrough in 1913, who, the following season, were to finish third in the English First Division.

By this time, there was an increasing interest in football from the working-class milieu across the city. The footballing arm of SC Armin, founded in 1910 and located in the worker district of Westend, consisted to a much higher degree than most teams of skilled tradesmen and shopkeepers, foreshadowing the football boom amongst Munich's working classes in the 1920s and 1930s. August Meyer, who was involved in organising youth football, provides a memorable image of street football in 1910 Munich, though it could really have been describing almost any other city in Germany, or in Britain, for that matter:

> In all parts of the city, where only half-suitable places are available, even on public streets, one sees boys playing with a ball. And if there is not a ball, a ball made of rags, a ball of rubber, a round stone, a broken bottle, etc. etc. – almost anything that can be kicked with a foot. One rarely sees complete teams. Two, three and more boys just playing together, scoring goals with stones or rags; a goal is scored and the games goes on.

Such an image of football contentment, however, did not stop the game being banned in schools across Bavaria in January 1912 due the prevalence of injuries to pupils.

Football continued in Munich during the First World War on a regular – though hugely disrupted – basis, even through the Hunger Winter of 1916/17. Even the earth-shattering announcement of Germany's capitulation in November 1918 did not prevent games taking place. Neither did the immense political upheavals of 1918/19, which included the Bavarian Revolution, carried out in Munich, and its aftermath, including the assassination of Bavarian Minister President Kurt Eisner in February 1919 on the city's streets, nor the near-civil-war conditions of early-to-mid 1919. Indeed, two days after Eisner's assassination, with the city brimming with pro- and anti-revolutionary fervour, there was time for Bayern Munich to defeat the far from aptly named SC Eldorado 4-0 in a friendly game. Games continued during the following months, hardly pausing in the wake of more deaths following the declaration of the Munich Räterepublik on 7 April or the subsequent fleeing of Bavarian Minister President Johannes Hoffmann from the city with his government. As the death toll climbed, and as German government troops and right-wing Freikorps soldiers prepared to retake the city (and particularly in the case of the Freikorps take bloody reprisals), both 1860 and Bayern Munich played friendly games, as they did in the immediate aftermath of the successful military attack. During the night of 13 April, not yet quite at the height of the revolutionary violence, 17 people were killed. The same day, 1860 and Bayern Munich played out a 1-1 draw at Grünwalder Straße. And on 4 May, just as government troops had wrested back control of the city, Bayern played out a 2-2 draw with TV West München.

Football across Germany experienced a sharp upswing during the immediate post-war years, with rising club membership and increased attendances. League football in Munich was re-established in 1919/20, and initially the most popular and the most successful club was neither Bayern Munich nor 1860, but FC Wacker. But it was during the inter-war years that Bayern Munich began to establish itself as a footballing force to be reckoned with. Bayern's president, initially in 1913, then for most of the period between 1919 until 1933, was the businessman Kurt Landauer, who provided direction and focus to the club. Landauer's Jewish background is significant, and it seems that it was because of this, and the fact that two of the clubs founders, Gustav Manning and Josef Pollack, were also Jewish, that the club became known as a *Juden-Klub*, or 'Jewish club'. Landauer had great contacts and took the team on many foreign visits to play against top European teams, while he also invited some of Europe's top clubs to Munich. Even a 7-1 trouncing against the superb Magyar Testgyakorlók Köre of Hungary was to be celebrated as a great football occasion and praised as evidence that Munich was very much a football city. The *Münchner Neueste Nachrichten* report of the game concluded that football 'is the sport of the masses for the Munich population.' Match attendances began to boom, with crowds regularly reaching 10,000, before rising to 20,000 for a 1927 clash between Wacker and 1860, then 25,000 between Wacker and Bayern later in the same year.

As well as signing star players, Landauer signed up famous managers to coach the team, including Britons William Townley (1919 to 1921) and James

McPherson (1924 to 1927), the latter under whom in 1925/26 Bayern won the Bavarian Championship. Both Bayern and FC Wacker reached the final stages of the all-important German Championships in 1928, as 1860 had done the previous year, an era culminating in the most successful years for inter-war Munich football. In 1931, 1860 Munich reached the German Championship final, only to be 'unluckily' defeated 3-2 in the final in Cologne by Hertha Berlin. This far and away represented the best success thus far for the club, and in great football style, the referee, a Herr Fissenewerth, wrote his name into the history of the club as two of the Hertha goals were apparently 'offside'.

A year later, Bayern reached the final at nearby Nuremberg and goals from Oskkar Rohr and Franz Krumm were sufficient to secure a 2-0 win against Eintracht Frankfurt, and with it a first ever Munich triumph in the German Championship. As was the norm, thousands of jubilant fans invaded the pitch, while an estimated 100,000 greeted the team's arrival in Munich. In two years, including one final loss and one final victory, Munich had shown itself to be the undisputed strongest football city in Germany. But it could not last, though this had less to do with the cyclical nature of success in sport than it did with politics: a year later, club president, Kurt Landauer (along with the many other Jewish members of Bayern Munich), became *persona non grata* under the Nazi regime and was hounded out of the club. Furthermore, the labelling of the club as a 'Jewish club' deemed Bayern Munich politically unreliable.

For many years after 1945, few people were interested in discussing the Jewish background of Bayern Munich. In a fascinating piece for *Die Zeit* newspaper in 2003, however, journalist Heike Faller by-lined an article with the following sentence: 'Why there is indeed a reason to like Bayern Munich: the story of a club which supported its Jewish president.' After being relieved of his position as president of Bayern Munich, Landauer was eventually to spend many weeks in the nearby concentration camp at Dachau, before on 15 May 1939 he wisely fled to Gent, Switzerland. That Landauer eventually returned from exile at the end of the Third Reich to take over the club for a short time only adds piquancy to his story. The point of Faller's article was that although Landauer's story is fascinating, and although Bayern Munich seem to come out of it with some credit, hardly anyone in the city knows about the Jewish history of the club, though this is now changing: the official history of the club, for example, now applauds the work by 'the Bonn English professor and historian Heiner Gillmeister' for his research in detailing the role played in the club's existence by 'two Jewish football enthusiasts – Gustav "Gus" Manning and Josef Pollack.'

Similarly, football during the Third Reich is still relatively under-researched. Evidence suggests that after Landauer was forced out of his position at Bayern Muich in 1933, it was arguably only as late as April 1943 that a Nazi Party member could really take full control at the apex of the club. The contrast with 1860 Munich could not, it appears, have been starker, though it would be far too simplistic to declare a straightforward dichotomy depicting Bayern Munich as an anti-Nazi club and 1860 as a pro-Nazi club. There is, however, clear evidence to suggest that 1860 was an organisation with very close links to the Nazi Party. As shown by Anton Löffelmeier, the club had well-established connections throughout the 1920s to Nazi Party members. For example: Fritz Ebenböck had already joined the Nazi Party by 1922 and was a member of the brown-shirted SA, and as a participant in Hitler's Munich putsch attempt of 1923, he was considered part of an elite group of Hitler's 'Old Comrades'. Ebenböck served as president of 1860 Munich between 1934 and 1935 before being followed by Dr Ludwig Holzer, a long-time SA leader and another participant in the putsch attempt. Holzer was then replaced by Dr Emil Ketterer, member of 1860 since 1908, a member of the NSDAP since 1923 and a member of the Munich city council from April 1933. And Wilhelm Brückner, a Nazi Party member of the German parliament and a later adjutant of Adolf Hitler, was a member of 1860 Munich football club.

During the Third Reich it was 1860 that performed best out of the Munich clubs in the newly formed Bavarian Regional League, a title they won once, as they did the more prestigious South German Championship. They were, however, unable to make much impression nationally except for winning the German Cup three years into the Second World War, on 15 November 1942, in the Berlin Olympic Stadium in front of 80,000 fans.

With the Wehrmacht's devastating defeat at Stalingrad announced just a few months later and with Allied air attacks on German cities causing ever-greater damage, it started to become increasingly evident that Germany could not win the war. The destruction across the entire Reich from early 1942 to the war's end in May 1945 was immense. Among the chaos and bombed-out city of Munich, competitive football continued, though in a truncated manner, occasionally entailing players returning from the front to play, more often clubs taking players working in the nearby arms industries. Indeed, Bayern Munich players found time to lose an Upper Bavaria Cup game against Bajuwaren on 2 April 1945, who then went on to lose the final on 15 April against 1860 Munich. Bayern and 1860 played a friendly on 23 April, a week before Hitler committed suicide in his Berlin bunker, on 30 April, the same day US soldiers entered Munich. Even in these catastrophic times, the only thing that finally put a stop to football matches was a ban imposed on all sports by the US occupation authorities.

1860: Munich's Finest

In a West Germany transformed by the *Wirtschaftswunder*, with its capital in the slightly nondescript city of Bonn, and with Berlin divided and very much the centre of Cold War Europe, Munich was viewed in certain respects as Germany's pre-eminent cultural and sporting centre.

In the immediate post-war years, however, Munich was little different from other major cities in that to most people eking out an existence among the rubble was of paramount importance. Similar to the reconstitution of other areas of Munich cultural life, rebuilding sports clubs provided a valuable distraction to everyday trevails.

Unofficial games were organised within weeks of the arrival of US troops, though the first games for 1860 and Bayern Munich in the newly constituted Oberliga Süd (South German Championship) did not get the go-ahead to start until 4 November 1945. Neither of Munich's two major clubs set the football world alight in the early years of the post-war period, nor did the 1947 short-lived return of former president Kurt Landauer to Bayern make much difference to the club's distinctly average performances. In fact, the most discussed aspect of football in Munich at this time seems to have been the lack of adequate training facilities and the lack of adequate football stadiums in the city. Foreshadowing the seemingly perennial predicament of 1860 in the later decades of the 20th century, the club experienced the first of many relegations in 1953, though Bayern Munich hardly fared any better as they were also relegated in 1955. By the time of the 1954 welcome at Marienplatz for the victorious West Germany World Cup winning squad, it was clear that Munich football fans were in desperate need of something to cheer. The late 1950s finally heralded a much-needed change of fortune, starting in 1957 with a 1-0 Bayern Munich win against Fortuna Düsseldorf in the German Cup final, the second most prestigious honour in German domestic football, after the national championship.

Perhaps prophetically pointing towards the long-term future for both clubs, in the same year 1860 were deducted points for illegal payments to players, something certainly far from rare at the time. The Oberiga Süd was not strictly a professional league: players were paid to play, but with a restrictive salary cap of DM 400 maximum a month, though both Munich clubs paid in excess of this. The writing had been on the wall for the geographically divided league system across Germany for some time, and the era of semi-professional leagues at the top of German football was increasingly seen as something of an anachronism. This was highlighted, for example, when Ludwig Janda of 1860 signed for Italian team Fiorentina in November 1949 for the considerable fee of 30,000 marks and received a huge pay rise as a professional, which was compensation enough for the player making himself ineligible for the German national team. The reality was that by the 1950s the amateur spirit was all but dead, and many clubs were punished for illegal payments while many top players received enticing offers to play in Spain as well as in Italy, a move that would provide a secure income in an exceptionally short career. Though the German Football Association typically dragged its feet, financial realities plus a poor performance at the 1962 World Cup helped persuaded the organisation that professionalism was the only option.

The first ever Bundesliga season (i.e. national German league) kicked off with 16 clubs on 24 August 1963, and it included Munich 1860 as Oberiga Süd champions, but not city rivals Bayern. In truth, if results over the previous decades were important criteria for deciding the make-up of the new national league, 1860 were thankful that they chose an opportune moment to win the Oberiga Süd championship, as neither premier Munich clubs' histories could compare with the best in Germany.

The short-lived success of 1860 was based around relative stability (for once) at the top with president Adalbert Wetzel, a top-class trainer in Max Merkel and a group of talented players, most notably an eccentric and adored Yugoslavian

The first ever Bayern Munich-1860 Bundesliga derby, 1965

goalkeeper, Petar Radenkovic (from Belgrade) and much-troubled star striker Rudi Brunnenmeier. Characteristic of the hard manner in which Merkel pushed the players to perform, he famously told journalists, 'The players much prefer to see me leaving than arriving.' A reasonable season finish of 12th was followed in 1964 by a win in the German cup final against Eintracht Frankfurt. Around 15,000 1860 fans had made their way from Munich to Stuttgart's Neckarstadion to see the team win 2-0, the club's first major trophy since 1942. The added bonus this time was that by winning the cup, 1860 became the first Munich club to qualify for a European competition.

Surprisingly for a club without a great pedigree, the following season, 1965, 1860 went all the way to the European Cup Winners Cup final in London, succumbing 2-0 to a fine West Ham United team which included future 1966 England World Cup winners of the calibre of Bobby Moore, Martin Peters and Geoff Hurst. A fourth place in the now 18-club Bundesliga in the same season represented a terrific year for the club.

The team was refined for the following season with the signing of striker Friedhelm 'Timo' Konietzka from 1965 German cup winners, Borussia Dortmund. With the team flying high in the Bundesliga, a late season 3-0 derby defeat at the hands of Bayern opened the possibility of precipitating a collapse. With two games to go the title was a two-horse race between Borussia Dortmund and 1860, but behind the scenes the players were increasingly at odds with their hard-line manager, and whether the players could pull together for the final two games of the season was in serious doubt.

The fixture list had fantastically thrown together the two top teams for the penultimate game, in which 1860 scraped through away from home with goals form Rudi Brunnenmeier and captain Peter Grosser. A final day 1-1 home draw against Hamburg in front of around 44,000 fans meant 1860 had won the club's – and Munich's – first-ever Bundesliga title. Indicating how strong Munich football was at this time, Dortmund were only able to fend off Bayern Munich into third place on a goals quotient calculation, while Bayern comfortably won the German cup 4-2 against Meidericher SV.

Though 1860 followed the championship-winning season with a creditable second place in 1967, the high watermark for the club had passed. It was during this period, the late-1960s, that the trajectories of both big Munich clubs started to radically diverge. Over the next 40 years, Bayern Munich would become Germany richest and most successful club – on and off the pitch – while 1860 would lurch from crisis to crisis, interspersed with the odd high point.

The Rise & Rise of 'Brand Bayern'

As the the 2008/9 football season drew to a close, 1860 were once again in financial trouble, once again toying with relegation from the Second Bundesliga division to the regional leagues. They survived by three points.

A month or so earlier, Bayern Munich, had been knocked out of football's premier club competition, the European Champions League, and manager Jürgen Klinsmann was losing popularity as quickly as he was losing players' and fans' confidence. Though Bayern Munich were a just few points off the top of the Bundesliga and in with a reasonable chance of winning the league, fans were voicing their displeasure, week by week, ever-more loudly. Klinsmann was sacked. It was normal for 1860 to be in turmoil, but Bayern Munich?

Except there was no crisis, explains Philipp Lahm, Bayern Munich full back. It was late April 2009 and Klinsmann had been sacked the day before. Lahm

Bayern Munich players featured prominently in the German side that won the 1974 football World Cup (above): captain Franz Beckenbauer (right with trophy), goalkeeper Sepp Maier (top, second left), striker Gerd Müller (top, fourth from left), Paul Breitner (top, third from right) Georg Schwarzenbeck (top, second right) and Uli Honess (bottom, far left)

strolled into the conference room as relaxed and as courteous as ever. He had every reason to be. He was utterly confident that even in the medium term, the club was in fine fettle. The reason? History, tradition and stability at the top. 'With 1860,' says Lahm, 'the problem is that as well as many changes of manager, there have also been problems at the top of the club, the board, the president. With Bayern, the top of the club stays the same.'

Ever since a certain Franz Beckenbauer teamed up in the mid-1960s with the likes of star striker Gerd Müller, goalkeeper Sepp Maier and initially under the tutelage of Yugoslav manager Zlatko 'Tschik' Cajkovski (appointed in 1963) and the presidency of Wilhelm Neudecker, Bayern have invariably been Germany's top club. By far the majority of the club's trophies have been won since the club's rise in the mid-1960s, and the club's success is a country mile ahead of any other club in Germany. The club has won a record 20 Bundesliga titles; a record 14 German cups; and a German record of four European Cups, bettered across Europe only by Real Madrid, AC Milan and Liverpool.

The most talented young footballers across the city are obviously much in demand by talent scouts from both Bayern and 1860, but the contest between whether the best sign for 'regional club' 1860 or the world-renowned club Bayern Munich is often hardly a contest worthy of the description: the cream of the city's young footballers generally turn up at Bayern. It is not only the success of Bayern Munich, however, that draws the best young players. 1860's seemingly perennial financial fiascos, the occasional acts of illegality and incompetence at the top of the club's hierarchy are hardly a great attraction. Indeed, one of the club's board members was imprisoned for financial irregularities related to the building of the Allianz Arena football stadium, which was until recently owned by both clubs. Indeed, Bayern Munich bought out the financially stricken 1860's 50-per-cent share for 11 million euros shortly after the stadium was built, although the latter have an option of buying back these shares in the unlikely scenario that the club should have the available funds. Moreover, as local Munich newspapers often highlight, many (not all) 1860 fans are more concerned with a return to their old Grünwalder Stadion, rejecting the Allianz Arena completely, perceiving it to be Bayern Munich's ground.

This is also part of the self-perception that 1860 are the city's true 'traditional' club, with fans originating from within the city, while Bayern are the nouveau rich cousins, whose fans are not real Münchners. Munich born and raised football journalist Raphael Honigstein is a writer on English football for the *Süddeutsche Zeitung* and also a writer on German football for British newspaper the *Guardian*. Honigstein strongly disagrees with the notion of 1860 representing a more authentic Munich club: 'People will tell you that in the city of Munich there are more 1860 fans. And that many Bayern fans come from the surrounding areas, which I think is true, because in absolute numbers there are many more Bayern Munich fans. But I think that if you were to go from house to house within Munich and ask: "Who do you support?" I think Bayern would have a majority.' He contends that 1860 'are a very strange club. Lots of in-fighting, disaffection, one fan group fighting the other. It's been like that for ever. And very mismanaged.' Few neutral observers disagree.

Contemporary success for Bayern is much more than winning the Bundesliga and competing in the Champions League. The club is backed by huge financial resources and a brand name that no other club in Germany comes close to matching. Regardless of current success or otherwise, Bayern Munich are a footballing powerhouse and in many regards sit in the same bracket as, for example, Manchester United and Liverpool (England), Barcelona and Real Madrid (Spain), and AC Milan, Inter Milan and Juventus (Italy). The difference is that while England, Spain and Italy have at least two clubs with a genuine worldwide appeal, Germany has just one: Bayern Munich, and with it comes the concomitant attention from various national and international media organisations.

Though current domestic German football is seen as somewhat below the level in the top two European leagues of England and Spain – and, according to UEFA's five-year statistics of results, similar to Italy's Serie A – financially Bayern Munich are capable of competing with the best, and, unlike most clubs in these leagues, the club does not carry huge and unsustainable debt. Bayern, however, have (at least until recently) a reputation as a club reluctant to spend on a scale currently associated with English and Spanish clubs. The yearly football financial report from Deloitte that ranks clubs according to their revenues, released in 2009 for the 2007/8 football season, puts Bayern Munich (295.3 million euros) in fourth place, behind Real Madrid (365.8m euros), Manchester United (324.8 million euros) and Barcelona (308 million euros). Though the Bundesliga is behind England and Spain in TV deals, the increasing success of the business side of Bayern Munich can be gauged from the fact that in a season when the team had not qualified for the lucrative Champions League (losing 19 per cent of expected TV revenue), the club increased its commercial revenues by a huge 69.3 million euros (up 65 per cent). This commercial revenue represents 60 per cent of the total revenue of the club and is around 45 million euros higher than Real Madrid, the second highest commercial earner in European football for 2007/8. As highlighted in the report, this significant increase in earning power is down to a number of factors, most notably the effect of Bayern

Philipp Lahm, born and raised in Munich

buying out Munich 1860's stake in the Allianz Arena football stadium. This provides the club with 41.6 million euros a year in revenue streams. Another source of income that has risen sharply, again highlighting the further raised profile of the club in recent seasons, is that sales of club merchandising rose by 27 per cent (8.8 million euros) to 11.1 million euros. Sponsorship revenues (notably Deutsche Telekom, plus adidas, which also owns 10 per cent of the club) brought in 74.3 million euros (up 11.5 million euros). Finally, home matches generated 69.4 million euros for the club.

Franz Beckenbauer lifting the 1974 European Cup

The impact of a strong Bayern Munich on the image of the city of Munich is immense. For some people around the world, Munich may be about lederhosen and the Oktoberfest, for others it may be about high-tech businesses and low crime. But just as people link the word 'Manchester' to 'United' or 'Real' to 'Madrid', an increasing number of people around the world link 'Bayern' to 'Munich'. As the figures above reveal, 'Bayern Munich' is a world-class brand.

In the March and April weeks prior and immediately after Jürgen Klinsmann's sacking the media seemed to be going into some kind of collective meltdown in their efforts to portray Bayern as a club with a problem. While not suggesting that Bayern Munich are inured to the cyclical nature of success, Philipp Lahm understands the status Bayern Munich holds all too well, which is why he could nonchalantly bat away questions about a 'club in turmoil' or any comparison with the seemingly crisis-ridden 1860. 'What has happened below, with managers and trainers, is pretty normal,' he explains. It would be better 'if Bayern had a situation such as Sir Alex Ferguson at Manchester United', he concedes. Someone 'who has stayed at his club as manager for years. But here we have Uli Hoeness.'

It would difficult to over-estimate the role Uli Hoeness has played in the success of the club. Injury in his prime cut short what had been a brilliant playing career with Bayern. Now club president, until recently he held the position of deputy chairman of Bayern's executive board, though this hardly revealed his real influence. Until 2009, during Bayern Munich games, as is traditional in German football, he sat on the bench next to the 'trainer'. His post-match combative interviews endeared him to few people outside Munich and he is possibly the most disliked person in German football while managing to be at the same time the person most fans would love to have running their club.
Hoeness, however, is only one part of a triumvirate (in the public's eyes, at least) at the top of Bayern Munich, the other two being Karl-Heinz Rummenigge, chairman of the executive board (of the business arm of the club) and honoury club president (and chairman of the supervisory board) Franz Beckenbauer.
Raphael Honigstein explains that Bayern Munich 'is a club that in a sense was taken over by a small group of players. A club that was still very parochial and provincial in a way, and they made it into a worldwide brand in the space of 10-15 years. It really starts in the 1960s, when Bayern start to emerge with Beckenbauer, then Hoeness came and Rummenigge a bit later. And they're still around now.'
Honigstein cites Thomas Hüetlin, whose excellent book *Gute Freunde: Die Wahre Geschichte des FC Bayern München* describes how a handful of players, helped create, as Honigstein describes it, a 'unique club'. Beckenbauer, Hoeness and Rummenigge are all great former Bayern Munich players. But while Hoeness and Rummenigge today have considerable influence on how the club is run, it is Beckenbauer, with far less 'official' influence, who is most revered, who stands at the top as not just the greatest Bayern player, but arguably Germany's greatest player.
A recent book about football in Munich starts with the sentence: 'Whoever wants to write about football in Munich has to start with Beckenbauer.' It goes on to state, 'Today, everybody in the whole world knows him, and he sits alongside Pelé in the hall of football fame.' If the former is arguable, the latter is most certainly true. Born in Giesing, Beckenbauer famously refused to contemplate playing for 1860 after being insulted by one of the club's players when playing a youth game for SC 1906. Beckenbauer has since described how 1860 at that time were 'my club', the team all of his team-

Built for the 1972 Olympics, the Olympic Stadium's major use for over 30 years was as the home of Bayern Munich and 1860. At the same time, the huge expenditure on the wider Olympic complex has been largely justified by its – on the whole – extensive use up to the present day

mates had dreamed of playing for. The oft-repeated story is that when Beckenbauer looked at an opposition player, the player said: 'What do you want, idiot?' Beckenbauer was incensed and did the only thing he knew how: he tore into the opposition, scored a goal and retorted, 'Now look, idiot!' But the youngsters of 1860 prevailed and the player returned after the game to the angry Beckenbauer with a few more taunts, once again calling him an 'idiot'. He chose to join Bayern Munich and the rest, as they say, is history. Similarly, contemporary Bayern player Philipp Lahm cites his father's influence on him as to why he always preferred Bayern Munich over 1860, who he actually turned down: 'I got an offer at 11 years of age from 1860 Munich,' he explains, laughing. 'I didn't go there for one reason: I went for a trial and behind the goal in the netting was a hole. I said to my mother, "I'm not going in there. There's a hole in the net." And a year later, Bayern asked whether I wanted to join them. And I went to Bayern.'

While faulty netting may seem a minor reason not to join one club over another, it is indicative of not only the attention to detail of top clubs, but also the power 'brand' Bayern Munich holds: such a wealthy club as Bayern Munich, one would presume, would not have damaged goal nets. So, Franz Beckenbauer joined Bayern rather than 1860 over an insult; around four decades later, Philipp Lahm did the same because of the state of the nets. In short, given a choice, the best young talent in Munich invariably choose the wealthier and more successful Bayern Munich.

Franz Beckenbauer's brilliance was to (re)invent the role of sweeper, a position at the centre of the defence, by using his great football technique and vision to both defend and then launch attacks. He was integral to the superb Bayern Munich teams that won the European Cup three times in a row in 1974, 1975 and 1976, victories that cemented Bayern's reputation as one of Europe's great clubs, and importantly provide the stones of history on which the club's stability has been built upon to the present day.

While in many regards Beckenbauer is the unofficial – perhaps for many non-Bayern fans, the acceptable – public face of Bayern Munich, his captaining (1974) and later managing of the German national side to World Cup winning success (1990) meant he was the obvious choice to be the public face of the hugely successful 2006 World Cup held in Germany. It is an interesting aside that while Raphael Honigstein agrees that while Beckenbauer's reputation within Germany can occasionally veer a touch into the realm of 'figure of fun', such was the admiration for Beckenbauer during the 2006 World Cup that there was almost 'the feeling he was the German president,' he says. He recounts a newspaper article during the tournament about how Beckenbauer, 'despite all his flaws, if he had chosen to stand for president, would have have stood a very good chance. He's got that charm and wit. He never comes across as arrogant. He's the kind of guy who walks into a room and shakes everybody's hand and makes them believe that he is genuinely pleased to meet them. But it does not feel contrived. You look at his face and he seems genuinely happy to meet you.'

Bayern Munich won their first Bundesliga title in 1969, and for a second time in 1972. While Bayern were evolving into Germany's biggest club, and laying the foundations for what would become 'brand Bayern', 1972 was the year the club, along with 1860 Munich, moved into its new playing arena: the

Olympic Stadium, built for the 20th Olympic Games in Munich. It proved to be enough of an inspiring football stadium for Bayern Munich to hammer title rivals Schalke 04 5-1 in their first ever game there, all but ending the title race in favour of Bayern.

Even with the caveat that the stadium never really satisfactorily fulfilled its football remit by being much more of an athletics arena, it was undoubtedly an inspired design. The Olympic complex was built on the rubble cleared away after the destruction of Munich by Allied bombing raids in the Second World War. Stadium architects, Günter Behnisch (whose architectural practice was responsible for coming up with the overall Olympic area concept) and Frei Otto had an additional responsibility to ensure that not only was the design of a high quality, but that the stadium had to be seen to be light years away from anything that could be construed as having Nazi connotations, meaning in particular nothing 'monumental'. Coming just 27 years after the fall of the Third Reich, Germany was still firmy embedded in a phase of rehabilitation in the eyes of a still suspicious West.

No different to all Olympics in having political aims, the games themselves followed tight political parameters. As shown by Eva Maria Modrey, the conception of the Munich games was intentionally conceived to be in stark contrast to the former Nazi dictatorship in three ways: the games were to be as far removed from the 1936 Nazi-era Berlin Olympics as possible; they had to somehow reflect opposition to National Socialism in general; and they should accentuate the positive Germany, that of the democratic West Germany, as opposed to communist East Germany. Quite a task for one three-week sporting event.

The radically avant-garde sweeping roof canopy atop the Olympic Stadium, seemingly anchored to the ground by thick steel cables, wonderfully winds its way to cover the other principal sports arenas in the Olympic complex. This, added to the Olympic Stadium's airy and open design concept, were seen as fundamental elements in accentuating an image of a modern and democratic West Germany. Though not without a handful of critics, and massively over budget (the total cost was possibly as high as 1.35 billion Deutsche marks), the Olympic complex was overwhelmingly praised as a wonderful creation. Moreover, by most estimates, the attempt to convey a democratic and contra-Nazi-Germany message was deemed to be largely successful, with the Boston-

The design of the Olympic Stadium (notably the roof) was seen as manifesting an image of an open and democratic Germany

based *Christian Science Monitor* capturing the mood, reporting that, 'The roof can be understood as a symbol for Germans' position in the world: modern, economically stabilised and cosmopolitan.'

The subsequent kidnap and murder of 17 Israeli athletes from the Munich Olympic village, however, inevitably overshadowed the positive image the games had garnered for the city. As much as contemporary visitors to Munich are impressed with the still much-liked and much-used Olympic complex, they equally associate the location with the tragedy more so since the release of Steven Spielberg's film loosely based on the terrible events. The name of the film is simply: *Munich*.

Two years later, the same year that Bayern Munich started a run of three successful European Cup triumphs, Franz Beckenbauer captained the West German national side to its second World Cup win, the final being held on 7 July 1974 at Munich's Olympic Stadium. West Germany's victory endeared them to few people outside the country as they beat the so-called 'Total Football' side of the Netherlands 2-1. That the German team was far better on the day has been conveniently ignored. Three decades later, Berlin, now the capital of a unified Germany, was the obvious choice to hold the final of the 2006 football World Cup. Similar to a World Cup being the driving force in the building of Munich's Olympic Stadium in 1972, the 2006 event propelled the city to build the incomparable Allianz Arena, the current shared home of 1860 and Bayern, designed by architecture firm Herzog & de Meuron.

The 'futuristic' near 70,000 all-seater stadium, located north of the city centre at Fröttmaning, with its 2,874 inflated polymer roof panels that glow with the red of Bayern or the blue of 1860 (depending on who is playing at home, with the further option of white for the German national team), has been described as resembling anything from a recently descended UFO to a giant bubble. The design concept alone is superb, but that it is located in 'conservative Munich', a city so often accused of looking backwards rather forwards architecturally, has been seen as doubly surprising. Just as the 1972 stadium was lavishly praised, so has the Allianz Arena. The architecture publication *The Arup Journal* starts its review of the building by stating, 'The Allianz Arena in Munich sets a new architectural milestone in stadium design.' Its concludes:

> Many consider the 1972 Munich Olympic Stadium, designed by Günter Behnisch, to be the best of its era. The Allianz Arena opened in May 2005 to critical acclaim as the city's second such example, not just for its innovative and iconic appearance but also for the excellent viewing and great atmosphere in its viewing bowl. Interestingly, … it has often been described as [incorporating a] "British style", in spectator proximity and atmosphere, by the German press.

On the one hand, the stadium reflects the corporate world in which Bayern Munich comfortably move, and its name refers to the Allianz insurance and financial services concern, which is headquartered in Munich. On the other hand, a number of 1860 fans see do not see the need to share with Bayern, can afford to share with Bayern nor see the need for such an auspicious and grandiose stadium. Furthermore, this is even more true when one consid-

The Allianz Arena has been extensively praised for its innovative design, but a number of 1860 Munich fans are unhappy to have to call it 'home'

ers that 1860 are mired in mediocrity in the second Bundesliga division, have a history of mismanagement and have little prospect of attracting anywhere near 70,000 people to fill a ground many of the club's fans reject.

While it remains to be seen whether those 1860 fans demanding a return to their old 'Sechsger' (Grünwalder Stadion) ground will get their way, it is likely that it is going to take a major transformation of the club before any success on the field can be countenanced. In contrast, in a football world where only the rich prosper like never before, it is Bayern Munich, with their well-established tradition of success and the millions garnered from huge sponsorship deals, not forgetting ever-greater exposure from untapped markets in Asia and Africa, that should tread the smoother path to greater glory. But a word of warning is perhaps worth sounding. Critics point out that not all supporters (across the European leagues) want the razzamatazz that goes with shiny new stadiums and huge TV deals. As the city of Munich exemplifies, olde worlde tradition is not necessary a bad thing. Though undoubtedly difficult to resist, critics argue that surely not every club has to buy into the new corporate vision of football.

Moreover, the all-singing and all-dancing 'brand Bayern' Munich of today is a far cry from the club of 50 years ago. And in the 1980s, just as in Britain, football was nowhere near the TV saturation sport it is today. There is, then, no guarantee that in 30 years time the Allianz Arena will not be playing host to Bayern Munich in front of 20,000 lonely supporters. And it would certainly feel a lot cosier in the tightly packed Grünwalder Stadion. In the meantime, it is 'brand Bayern', immutably linked around the world to the city of Munich, that adds an extra layer of star quality to the city's reputation.

Select Bibliography

For a full list see www.paul-wheatley.eu

Albrecht, Günter, *Königlicher Braukunst. Die Wittelsbacher und das Bier* (Rosenheim, 2006)

Altmann, Lothar, *Streifzüge durch Münchens Kunstgeschichte. Von der Romantik bis zur Gegenwart* (Schnell + Steiner)

Assel, Astrid & Christian Huber, *München und das Bier* (Volk Verlag, 2009)

Bauer, Richard, *Geschichte Münchens* (Munich, 2005)

Bauer, Richard, & Fritz Fenzl, *175 Jahre Oktoberfest 1810-1985* (Bruckmann, 1985)

Berghahn, Volker R., *Imperial Germany 1871-1918. Economy, Society, Culture and Politics* (Oxford 2005)

Biller, Josef H., & Hans-Peter Rasp, *München. Kunst & Kultur* (Südwest Verlag, 2005)

Brown, G. I., *Scientist, Soldier, Statesman, Spy. Count Rumford* (Sutton Publishing, 2001)

Denzel, Markus A., *Geschichte des Finanzplatzes München* (Oldenbourg Verlag, 2007)

Evans, Richard J., *The Third Reich in Power* (London, 2005)

Flügel, Rolf (ed), *Lebendiges München* (Verlag F. Bruckman, 1958)

Fulbrook, Mary, *A Concise History of Germany* (Cambridge University Press, 2000)

Jefferies, Matthew, *Imperial Culture in Germany, 1871-1918* (Palgrave Macmillan, 2003)

Jerram, Leif, *Germany's Other Modernity. Munich and the Making of Metropolis, 1895-1930* (Manchester University Press, 2007)

Grunberger, Richard, *Red Rising in Bavaria* (Arthur Barker, 1973)

Hajak, Stefanie, & Zarusky, Jürgen (eds), *München und der Nationalsozialismus. Menschen. Orte. Strukturen.* (Metropol, 2008)

Hartmann, Claus, *Bayerns Weg in die Gegenwart. Vom Stammesherzogtum zum Freistaat heute* (Verlag Friedrich Pustet, 200X)

Hartmann, Claus, *Münchens Weg in die Gegenwart. Von Heinrich dem Löwen zur Weltstadt* (Verlag Schnell & Steiner, 2008)

Hausenstein, Wilhelm, *Liebe zu München* (Prestel Verlag, 1967)

Hesse-Lichtenberger, Ulrich, T*or! The Story of German Football* (London, 2003)

Hettler, Friedrich H. & Sing, Achim (eds), *Die Münchner Oberbürgermeister. 200 Jahre gelebte Stadtgeschichte* (Volk Verlag, 2008)

Heydenreuter, Reinhard, *Kleine Münchner Stadtgeschichte* (Regensburg, 2007)

Howitt, Anna Mary, *An Art-Student in Munich* (University of Michigan, 2005)

Hübner, Reinhard, *Münchner Fußball Gschichtn. Menschen, Mythen und Momente* (Wilhelm Heyne Verlag, 2008)

Hüetlin, Thomas, *Gute Freunde. Die Wahre Geschichte des FC Bayern München* (Munich, 2008)

Kershaw, Ian, *Hitler. 1889-1936 Hubris* (Penguin, 1998)

Kershaw, Ian, *Hitler. 1936-1945 Nemesis* (Penguin, 2000)

Robin Lenman, *Artists and Society in Germany, 1850-1914* (Manchester University Press, 1997)

Landeshauptstadt München, *München wie Geplant. Die Entwicklung der Stadt von 1158 bis 2008* (2008)

Large, David Clay, *Where Ghosts Walked. Munich's Road to the Third Reich* (W. W. Norton and Company, 1997)

Leutheusser, Ulrike and Heinrich Nöth (eds), *München leuchtet für die Wissenschaft. Berühmte Forscher und Gelehr*te [Band I and Band II] (Alitera Verlag, 2007/8)

Löffelmeier, Anton, *Die "Löwen" unterm Hakenkreuz. Der TSV München von 1860 im Nationalsozialismus* (Göttingen, 2009)

Löw, Konrad, *Die Münchner und ihre jüdischen Mitbürger 1900-1950 im Urteil der NS-Opfer und –Gegner* (Munich, 2008)
Makela, Maria, *The Munich Secession. Art and Artists in Turn-of-the-Century Munich* (Princeton University Press, 1990)
Metzger, Rainer, *Munich, Its Golden Age of Art and Culture 1890-1920* (Thames & Hudson, 2009)
Milosch, Mark S., *Modernizing Bavaria. The Politics of Franz Josef Strauß and the CSU, 1949-1969* (Berghahn Books, 2006)
Neumann Adrian, *Edda & Michael, Architektur und Kunst. München* (Stuttgart, 2009)
Prater, Donald, *Thomas Mann. A Life* (Oxford University Press, 1995)
Rosenfeld, Gavriel D., *Munich and Memory. Architecture, Monuments, and the Legacy of the Third Reich* (University of California Press, 2000)
Schostack, Renate, *Die Eitle Schöne. Über Geist und Kultur in München* (Sankt Michaelsbund, 2008)
Stahleder, Helmuth, *Chronik der Stadt München. Herzogs- und Bürgerstadt 1157-1505* (Dölling und Galitz Verlag, 1995)
Stahleder, Helmuth, *Chronik der Stadt München. Belastungen und Bedrückungen. Die Jahre 1506-1705* (Dölling und Galitz Verlag, 1995)
Stahleder, Helmuth, *Chronik der Stadt München. Erzwungener Glanz. Die Jahre 1706-1818* (Dölling und Galitz Verlag, 1995)
Statistisches Amt der Stadt München 1954, *Statistisches Handbuch der Stadt München* (Munich, 1954)
Tomlinson, Alan & Young, *Christopher, German Football. History, Culture, Society* (Oxford, 2006)

Photo Credits

akg: pages 26/27, 55, 57, 61, 150/151, 169
artothek: page 65
Bayerisches Nationalmuseum: pages 29
Bayerische Schlösserverwaltung: page 43 (Philip Mansmann)
Bayerisches Hauptstaatsarchiv: page 12
BMW: page 144
Brandl, Anton: page 149
Der Spiegel: page 98
Deutsches Museum: pages 111, 122, 123
FC Bayern: page 205
Fotolia: pages 36, 40, 132, 155, 157
G. Sedlmayr Spaten-Franziskaner-Bräu KGaA: page 184
Wilfried Hösl/TAM: page 153
istock: pages 45, 83
Mullersches Volksbad: page 163
Munich Stadtmuseum: pages 106, 178, 187
Porzellan Manufaktur Nymphenburg: page 109
Shutterstock: pages 14, 103, 138, 147, 208, 211, 213
Stadtarchiv München: pages 69, 70, 77, 85, 99, 100, 141, 191
SZ Photo: pages 48, 86, 90, 96, 115, 126, 133, 201, 203, 206
Ullstein Bild: pages 73, 82, 166
Volk Verlag: pages 19 right, 146
Wheatley, Paul: pages 19 left, 23, 159, 174, 175

Index